Chet Baker in Europe

Chet Baker in Europe

1975 - 1988

Herausgegeben und
gestaltet von /
Edited and designed by
Ingo Wulff

Nieswand
Verlag

CD-Diskographie/CD discography

Burkhard Schiller, Bremen

Fotografien von/Photographs by

Belgien/Belgium
Philippe Gielen, Liège
Jacky Lepage, Dinant

Dänemark/Denmark
Jørgen Bo, Vordingborg
Andreas Johnsen, København
John R. Johnsen, København
Kirsten Malone, København
Gorm Valentin, København

Deutschland/Germany
David Baltzer, Berlin
Bernd Bingler, Aurach
Thilo Corts, Göttingen
Thomas Deutschmann, Hannover
Uwe Killing, Hamburg
Harald Koch, Hannover
Hans Kumpf, Murr
Ralph Quinke, Hamburg
Niels Schubert, Stuttgart
Manfred Rinderspacher, Mannheim
Michael Steen, Hamburg
Thomas Stolper, Frankfurt
Hyou Vielz, Köln
Josef Werkmeister, München
Ingo Wulff, Kiel

Finnland/Finland
Timo Pylvänäinen
(Lehtikuva Oy), Helsinki

Frankreich/France
Michel Becret, Paris
Philippe Cibille, Montreuil
Richard Dumas, Rennes
José Madani, Paris
Thierry Nectoux, Paris
Christian Rose, Paris
Ariane Smolderen, Paris

Großbritannien/Great Britain
Jak Kilby, London
Allan Titmuss, Surrey

Island/Iceland
Ingimundur Magnússon, Reykjavík

Italien/Italy
Fabrizio Biamonte, Roma
Luisa Cairati, Bergamo
Elena Carminati, Treviglio
Paolo Ferraresi, Rodano
Nino Leotta, Acireale
Marcello Mencarini, Roma
Carlo Pieroni, Tolentino
Giuseppe Pino, Milano
Gian Carlo Roncaglia, Torino
Carlo Verri, Robbiate

Kroatien/Croatia
Mladen Mazur, Zagreb

Niederlande/Netherlands
Hajo Piebenga, Rotterdam
Gert de Ruyter, Amsterdam
Barbara Walton (ap), Amsterdam

Norwegen/Norway
Randi Hultin, Oslo

Schweden/Sweden
Roland Bengtsson, Helsingborg
Gunnar Holmberg, Västerås
Dan Kjellman, Göteborg

Schweiz/Switzerland
Dany Gignoux, Genève

Spanien/Spain
Federico Gonzáles, Madrid

Texte von/Texts by

Belgien/Belgium
Jacques Pelzer, Liège
Jean-Louis Rassinfosse, Bruxelles
Philip Catherine, Bruxelles

Dänemark/Denmark
Jesper Lundgaard, København
Doug Raney, København
Niels-Henning Ørsted Pedersen, Ishøj

Deutschland/Germany
Rocky Knauer, Schwabmünchen
Wolfgang Lackerschmid, Ehingen

Frankreich/France
Riccardo Del Fra, Paris
Michel Graillier, Paris
Micheline Pelzer-Graillier, Paris

Italien/Italy
Enrico Pieranunzi, Roma
Enzo Pietropaoli, Roma

Niederlande/Netherlands
Edu Ninck Blok, Bilthoven
Hein Van de Geyn, Breda
Evert Hekkema, Amsterdam

Norwegen/Norway
Randi Hultin, Oslo

USA
Jon Burr, New York
Diane Vavra, Ben Lomond

Umschlagfoto / Cover photo
Roland Bengtsson

Frontispiz / Frontispiece
Philippe Cibille

Impressum / Imprint

© Nieswand Verlag
Kiel 1993
All rights reserved

Übersetzung / Translation
Caroline Mähl
englisch – deutsch / english – german
deutsch – englisch / german – english
Klemens Berthold
französisch – deutsch / french – german
Giuseppe de Siati
italienisch – deutsch / italian – german
Margret Brown
englisch – deutsch / english – german

Lektor / Reader
Inge-B. Berthold

Gestaltung / Design
Ingo Wulff

Lithografie / Reproduktion
Brandner, Kiel

Herstellung / Production
Nieswand Druck, Kiel
Satz / Typesetting
Hanne Sothen
Druckformen / Printing formes
Oliver Grabowsky
Druck / Print
Lars Fenner
Dieter Fernberg
Manfred Masuth

Bindung / Binding
Gehring, Bielefeld

Schrift / Typeface
Gill Sans

Papier / Paper
Gelblich weiß Spezial-Offset, 140 g / qm

Printed in Germany
ISBN 3-926048-57-3

Dank an / Thanks to

Bülent Ates
Erik van den Berg
Inge-B. Berthold
Klemens Berthold
Edu Ninck Blok
Kjeld Bülow
Richard Cook
Lars Fenner
Dieter Fernberg
Bertrand Fevre
Gerd Filtgen
Klaus D. Francke
Oliver Grabowsky
Cengiz Hadimli
Wolfram Knauer
Walter Lachenmann
Wolfgang Lackerschmid
Caroline Mähl
Kristján Magnússon
Leonard Malone
Manfred Masuth
Jens Nieswand
Jacques Pelzer
Micheline Pelzer-Graillier
Adrian von Ripka
Burkhard Schiller
Giuseppe de Siati
Ib Skovgaard
Hanne Sothen
Christina Sperenza
Gerry Teekens
Ove Tranekjær
Mehmet Ulug
Jeroen de Valk
Larry B. Whitford

& Bettina Wulff

Bildnachweis/Photo credits

David Baltzer 154[2]
Michel Becret 114
Roland Bengtsson 152, 153
Fabrizio Biamonte 54, 57, 135[2]
Bernd Bingler 83[2]
Jørgen Bo 28, 29, 52, 70
Luisa Cairati 15, 19, 23
Elena Carminati 87, 88, 94[2], 95
Philippe Cibille 2, 77, 78, 122[2],
    124, 134, 155
Thilo Corts 105
Cumhuriyet archive 128
dpa 173
Thomas Deutschmann 166
Richard Dumas 136, 137
Paolo Ferraresi 44, 46, 47, 49
Philippe Gielen 25, 76, 107, 163
Dany Gignoux 40, 41, 42, 43, 58, 59
Federico Gonzáles 73[2]
Gunnar Holmberg 26, 72, 76, 81, 82,
    90[2], 96, 101
Randi Hultin 29, 43, 74, 154
Andreas Johnsen 147[2]
John R. Johnsen 71
Jak Kilby 37, 38, 39[2], 63
Uwe Killing 129
Dan Kjellman 75
Harald Koch 100, 146
Hans Kumpf 26, 32, 33, 34
Jacky Lepage 107, 108/109, 110, 111[2],
    112, 113[2], 115, 130, 131, 132, 133
Nino Leotta 97[2]
José Madani 138, 141
Ingimundur Magnússon 89[2]
Kirsten Malone 148, 149[2], 150, 151[2]
Mladen Mazur 100[2]
Marcello Mencarini 67[2]
Thierry Nectoux 65[2]
Hajo Piebenga 119, 168[2], 171
Carlo Pieroni 23, 96, 102, 125, 156, 157,
    159[2]), 160[2]
Giuseppe Pino 16, 17
Timo Pylvänäinen (Lehtikuva Oy/dpa) 117
Ralph Quinke 53, 64, 166
Manfred Rinderspacher 57, 58, 61, 62
Gian Carlo Roncaglia 13, 14[2], 21, 22, 165
Christian Rose 19, 36, 70, 79
Gert de Ruyter 93, 126, 127
Niels Schubert 164[2]

Ariane Smolderen 139, 140, 162[2]
Michael Steen 116, 142[2]
Thomas Stolper 143
Allan Titmuss 104, 117, 118[2]
Gorm Valentin 27, 50, 51, 91, 92[2]
Carlo Verri 45[2], 54
Hyou Vielz 123[2]
Barbara Walton (ap) 175
Josef Werkmeister 19
Ingo Wulff 158

Literatur/Bibliography

Paolo Boncampagni/Aldo Lastella
Chet Baker in Italia
Stampa Alternativa, Roma 1991

Hans Henrik Lerfeldt
Thorbjørn Sjøgren
Chet – The Discography of
Chesney Henry Baker
Tiderne Skifter, København 1985

Gérard Rouy
Chet Baker
Éditions du Limon, Paris 1992

Jeroen de Valk
Chet Baker
Oreos, Schaftlach 1991

Ingo Wulff
Chet Baker in Concert
Nieswand, Kiel 1989

Chet Baker in Europe 1975 - 1988

The American trumpet player Chet Baker died in the early morning of May 13, 1988. He was 58 years old. His death was caused by a fall from a second-storey window of the Prins Hendrik Hotel in Amsterdam, sometime between two and three in the morning. Rumours still circulate regarding the exact circumstances: the Dutch police believe it was an accidental death stemming from drug abuse, others speak of murder, still others consider suicide a plausible explanation. Another theory says that Chet Baker tried to climb the hotel façade to enter his locked room without having to pass the reception desk. It is probable, though, that the fall from the window took place without the involvement of others since the door to his room was locked from the inside.

Chet Baker's professional career began in 1952, the year he joined the Gerry Mulligan Quartet. His ascent was rapid – between 1953 and 1958 he repeatedly topped the polls of "Downbeat", "Metronome" and "Melody Maker" – his descent equally so, the result of drugs, imprisonment and, in 1968, a fist fight in which he lost several teeth and was forced to stop playing for a considerable time. In 1974 Chet Baker celebrated his comeback in yet another "reunion" with baritone saxophonist Gerry Mulligan in New York's Carnegie Hall. He returned to Europe, after a lengthy absence, in 1975. For him and for his American colleagues, Europe offered more favourable conditions than the motherland of jazz: the money was better, the audiences and critics receptive. In the years to follow, Europe became a new "home" for Chet Baker, the returns to America fewer and shorter. On those journeys, he usually visited his family (mother, wife and three children) in Yale, Oklahoma. In the 70s, singer Ruth Young accompanied Chet Baker on his European tours; by the early 80s, he was sharing life on the road with saxophonist Diane Vavra.

Belgian saxophonist Jacques Pelzer had befriended Chet in the mid-Fifties, and the

Der amerikanische Trompeter Chet Baker starb in den frühen Morgenstunden des 13. Mai 1988 im Alter von achtundfünfzig Jahren. Ursache war der Sturz aus einem Fenster im zweiten Geschoß des Prins-Hendrik-Hotels in Amsterdam nachts zwischen zwei und drei Uhr. Noch immer kursieren Gerüchte über die genauen Umstände: Die niederländische Polizei geht von einem unfreiwilligen Sturz unter Einfluß von Drogen aus, andere sprechen von Mord, aber auch Selbstmord wird in Betracht gezogen. Eine weitere Theorie besagt, Chet Baker habe versucht, an der Fassade emporzuklettern, um in sein verschlossenes Zimmer zu gelangen, ohne die Hotelrezeption passieren zu müssen. Es ist jedoch sehr wahrscheinlich, daß der Sturz aus dem Fenster ohne Zutun eines anderen erfolgte, da die Zimmertür von innen verschlossen war.

Im Jahre 1952 begann die professionelle Karriere Chet Bakers im Gerry Mulligan Quartet. Ebenso steil wie sein Aufstieg als mehrfacher Pollwinner von „Downbeat", „Metronome" oder „Melody Maker" in der Zeit von 1953 bis 1958 verlief später auch sein Abstieg: Drogen, Gefängnisstrafen und 1968 eine Schlägerei, bei der er mehrere Zähne verlor, was ihn zu einer darauffolgenden Spielpause zwang. 1974 feierte Chet Baker dann sein Comeback in der New Yorker Carnegie Hall bei einer erneuten „Reunion" mit dem Baritonsaxophonisten Gerry Mulligan. Nach längerer Zeit kam er 1975 wieder nach Europa. Für ihn und seine amerikanischen Kollegen herrschten hier weitaus angenehmere Bedingungen als im Mutterland des Jazz: Akzeptanz bei Publikum und Presse und höhere Gagen. Europa wurde in den darauffolgenden Jahren zu einer neuen „Heimat" für Chet Baker, die Rückkehr in die USA immer seltener und die dortigen Aufenthalte immer kürzer. In der Regel waren diese Reisen mit Besuchen bei seiner Familie (Mutter, Ehefrau und drei Kinder) in Yale/Oklahoma verbunden. In den ersten Jahren nach 1975 begleitete ihn die Sängerin Ruth Young auf seinen Tourneen durch Europa; mit Beginn der achtziger Jahre war die Saxophonistin Diane Vavra seine Lebensgefährtin und Tourneebegleiterin.

Schon seit Mitte der fünfziger Jahre existierte eine enge Freundschaft mit dem belgischen Saxophonisten Jacques Pelzer, die bis zu Bakers Tod andauerte. Pelzers Haus in Liège war ein ständiger Ruhepunkt für Chet Baker während seiner rastlosen Tourneen; hier hatte er auch seine wenigen privaten Besitztümer untergebracht. Jacques Pelzers Tochter Micheline organisierte viele Dinge im Alltag Chet Bakers und war häufig auf Konzertreisen anwesend. Micheline Pelzer ist Schlagzeugerin und die Frau des Pianisten Michel Graillier, mit dem Baker über zehn Jahre zusammenarbeitete.

In fast jedem europäischen Land hatte Chet Baker einige gute Freunde: Randi Hultin in Oslo, Ove Tranekjær und Hans Henrik Lerfeldt in Kopenhagen, Evert Hekkema in Amsterdam, Bertrand Fevre in Paris oder Paolo Piangiarelli in Macerata. Eine eigene Wohnung hatte Baker jedoch nie in Europa, fast unablässig war er unterwegs von einem Land zum anderen; zwischen den einzelnen Auftrittsorten lagen häufig unzumutbare Entfernungen. Erst im Frühjahr 1988 plante er, ein Haus am Stadtrand von Paris zu mieten, um sich dort mit Diane Vavra niederzulassen. Diese reiste Mitte Februar in die USA, blieb dort unerwartet länger als vereinbart und kehrte bis zu Chet Bakers Tod nicht nach Europa zurück.

Die beiliegende CD enthält bisher auf Compact Disc unveröffentlichte Studioaufnahmen: in der kleinen Formation im Duo mit dem Vibraphonisten Wolfgang Lackerschmid und im großen Ensemble als Gastsolist des Amstel Octets. Außerdem sind vier Interviewauszüge mit Chet Baker zu hören.

Der vorliegende Bildband zeigt Stationen aus dem musikalischen und privaten Bereich der für mein Empfinden bedeutendsten Schaffensphase Chet Bakers, die in Amerika allerdings wenig Beachtung gefunden hat. Über fünfzig Fotografen aus fast allen Ländern Europas sind mit ihren Bildern vertreten und repräsentieren so gleichzeitig ein Stück europäische Jazzfotografie. Zahlreiche Musikerkollegen erinnern sich, meist in eigens für dieses Buch geschriebenen Texten, an ihre Zeit mit dem wohl lyrischsten Trompeter des Jazz. Diesen Fotografen und Musikern gilt mein ganz besonderer Dank.

Ingo Wulff, April 1993

association continued until Baker's death. Pelzer's Liège home was a place where the trumpeter could rest and relax. He stored his few personal belongings there and returned frequently in the course of his endless tours. Jacques Pelzer's daughter Micheline organized many of Chet Baker's daily affairs and was often present at his concerts. She is a drummer, and the wife of pianist Michel Graillier who played with Baker for more than ten years.

Chet Baker had at least one good friend in almost every major European country: Randi Hultin in Oslo, Ove Tranekjær and Hans H. Lerfeldt in Copenhagen, Evert Hekkema in Amsterdam, Bertrand Fevre in Paris, Paolo Piangiarelli in Macerata. What he never had, however, was a home of his own; he was almost constantly on route between countries, often covering ridiculous distances to get from one gig to the next. In the spring of 1988 he decided finally to settle down and rent a house for himself and Diane Vavra on the outskirts of Paris. In mid-February, however, Diane Vavra went back to America, and did not return to Europe until after Chet Baker's death.

The enclosed CD contains studio recordings not previously available on Compact Disc: in the smallest of ensembles, the duo, with vibraphone player Wolfgang Lackerschmid and, in a larger line-up, as guest soloist with the Amstel Octet. Additionally, the CD includes four excerpts from interviews with Chet Baker.

The pictures in this book illustrate stages, both musical and private, of what I believe was Chet Baker's most important creative phase — a phase, however, which has met with little attention in America. More than fifty photographers from all over Europe have contributed their work, representing, at the same time, a chapter of European jazz photography. In the texts, mostly written specifically for this book, many musicians recall their time with the man who was, arguably, jazz's most lyrical trumpeter. To these photographers and musicians, my special thanks.

Abkürzungen/Abbreviations

Sämtliche Angaben in der von Burkhard Schiller zusammengestellten Diskographie beziehen sich ausschließlich auf Compact Discs aus dem Zeitraum von 1975 bis 1988. Sie sind in chronologischer Folge geordnet und berücksichtigen weder Kompilationen noch Angaben zur Titellänge oder dem jeweiligen Aufnahmeverfahren. Aufnahmen in Europa sind in gerader Schrift, außereuropäische Aufnahmen in kursiver Schrift gesetzt. Die in der Diskographie und den Bildunterschriften verwendete Abkürzungen werden nachfolgend erklärt.

The discography compiled by Burkhard Schiller includes only compact discs from the period 1975 to 1988. These are listed in chronological order. Compilations are not included, nor are details of track lengths or recording methods. European recordings are set in regular type, non-European recordings in italics. The following list explains abbreviations used in the discography and in picture captions.

acc	accordeon/Akkordeon
afl	alto flute/Altflöte
arr	arranger/Arrangeur
as	alto saxophone/Altsaxophon
b	bass/Baß
bcl	bass clarinet/Baßklarinette
bfl	bass flute/Baßflöte
bh	bariton horn/Baritonhorn
bs	bariton saxophone Baritonsaxophon
cl	clarinet/Klarinette
clav	clavinet/Clavinette
co	cornet/Kornet
cond	conductor/Dirigent
dr	drums/Schlagzeug
eb	electric bass/Elektrobaß
eg	electric guitar/Elektrogitarre
ep	electric piano/Elektrisches Klavier
fl	flute/Flöte
flh	fluegelhorn/Flügelhorn
frh	french horn/Waldhorn
g	guitar/Gitarre
keyb	keyboards/Tasteninstrumente
mar	marimba/Marimba
org	organ/Orgel
p	piano/Klavier
perc	percussion/Schlagwerk
sax	saxophones/Saxophone
ss	soprano saxophone Sopransaxophon
synth	synthesizer/Synthesizer
tp	trumpet/Trompete
tb	trombone/Posaune
ts	tenor saxophone/Tenorsaxophon
vib	vibraphone/Vibraphon
vl	violin/Violine
voc	vocal/Gesang

B	Belgium/Belgien
BR	Brazil/Brasilien
CDN	Canada/Kanada
CH	Switzerland/Schweiz
D	Germany/Deutschland
DK	Denmark/Dänemark
E	Spain/Spanien
F	France/Frankreich
GB	England/Großbritannien
I	Italy/Italien
IS	Iceland/Island
J	Japan/Japan
N	Norway/Norwegen
NL	Netherlands/Niederlande
S	Sweden/Schweden
SF	Finland/Finnland
TR	Turkey/Türkei
YUG	Yugoslavia/Jugoslawien

Cal.	California
Conn.	Connecticut
La.	Louisiana
N.J.	New Jersey
N.Y.	New York
Okla.	Oklahoma
Tex.	Texas

at	alternate take Alternative Aufnahme
it	incomplete take unvollständige Aufnahme
prob	probably/wahrscheinlich

Jim Hall
Concierto
CBS/Epic 450896-2
PolyGram 813 661-2
(USA) CBS/CTI CK 40807
(J) CTI K35Y-600
(J) King 24OE-6812

Chet Baker – tp
Paul Desmond – as on 1, 6
Jim Hall – g
Roland Hanna – p
Ron Carter – b
Steve Gadd – dr

Englewood Cliffs, N.J. (USA)
April 16/23, 1975
1 You'd be so nice to come home
2 The answer is yes
3 The answer is yes (at)
4 Two's Blues
5 Rock skippin'
6 Concierto de Aranjuez

The Fabulous Pescara Jam Sessions
1970-1975
(I) Philology W 96-2

Chet Baker – tp
Jean Lubin – p
Didier Levallet – b
Franco Manzecchi – dr

Pescara (I), July 13, 1975
2 Old folks
3 Stella by starlight (it)
4 Airegin (it)

Seven Faces Of Valentine
(I) Philology W 30-2

Chet Baker – tp
Kenny Drew – p
Larry Ridley – b
David Lee – dr

Pescara (I), July 14, 1975
3 My funny Valentine

Live In Paris 1960-63
Live In Nice 1975
(F) Esoldun FCD 123

Chet Baker – tp
Larry Ridley – b
Ray Mosca – dr

Nice (F), July 20, 1975
5 Witchcraft [For minors only]
6 Stella by starlight

Chet Baker – tp, voc on 10
Bob Mover – as
Larry Ridley – b
David Lee – dr

Nice (F), July 24, 1975
7 Dear old Stockholm
8 Mister B
9 I waited for you
10 There will never be another you

Pescara (I) · July 14, 1975
Gian Carlo Roncaglia

Pescara (I) · July 14, 1975
Gian Carlo Roncaglia

CB + Ruth Young
Pescara (I) · July 14, 1975
Gian Carlo Roncaglia

Umbria (I) · July 1975
Luisa Cairati

CB + Kenny Drew
Perugia (I) · July 1975
16 *Giuseppe Pino*

Perugia (I) · July 1975
Giuseppe Pino

Deep In A Dream Of You
(1) Moon MCD 026-2

Chet Baker – tp, voc on 3, 4
Jacques Pelzer – fl
Isla Eckinger – b
Harold Danko – p

Roma (I), Oct/Nov 1976
1 Tidal breeze
2 If you could see me now
3 Look for the silver lining
4 Deep in a dream of you
5 Chet's theme

CB + Jacques Pelzer
Dalmine (I)/Bobadilla Feling Club
Nov 1976
Luisa Cairati

Paris (F)/Palais de la Mutualité
Dec 1, 1976
Christian Rose

Berlin (D) · 1976
Josef Werkmeister

You Can't Go Home Again
A&M 396 997-2
(USA) A&M CD 0805
(J) A&M D32Y-3830
(J) A&M D22Y-3906
(J) Polygram POCM-5028

Chet Baker – tp
Michael Brecker – ts on 1, 2, 4
Paul Desmond – as on 3
Kenny Barron – ep on 3
Richie Beirach – ep, clav on 1, 2, 4
John Scofield – eg on 1, 2, 4
Ron Carter – b
Alphonso Johnson – eb on 1, 2
Tony Williams – dr
Ralph MacDonald – perc on 1, 4
Hubert Laws – fl, bfl, piccolo-fl on 2, 4
Don Sebesky – ep on 2, 3
John Campo – bassoon on 4
David Nadien, Rochelle Abramson,
Max Ellen, Paul Gershman, Diana Halprin,
Harold Kohon, Charles Libove,
Marvin Morgenstern, Matthew Raimondi –
strings on 1, 2, 4
Jesse Levy, Charles McCracken,
Alan Shulman – cello on 1, 2, 4

New York, N.Y. (USA)
Feb 16/21/22, May 13, 1977
1 Love for sale
2 Un poco loco
3 You can't go home again
4 El Morro

The Best Thing For You
A&M 397 050-2
(USA) A&M CD 0832
(J) A&M D22Y-3920
(J) Polygram POCM-5027

Chet Baker – tp, voc on 3, 4, 5
Michael Brecker – ts on 6
Paul Desmond – as on 2, 4
Richie Beirach – ep on 6
John Scofield – eg on 6
Ron Carter – b/out on 5
Kenny Barron – p/out on 5
Tony Williams – dr/out on 5
Hubert Laws – fl on 6
Arto Tuncboyachi – perc, voice on 6
Gene Bertoncini – g on 5

New York, N.Y. (USA)
Feb 16/21/22, May 13, 1977
1 The best thing for you
2 I'm getting sentimental over you/
You've changed
3 Oh, you crazy moon
4 How deep is the ocean
5 If you could see me now
6 El Morro

Once Upon A Summertime
Galaxy OJCCD-405-2
(F) Carrere 99.925

Chet Baker – tp
Gregory Herbert – ts
Harold Danko – p
Ron Carter – b
Mel Lewis – dr

New York, N.Y. (USA), Feb 20, 1977
1 Tidal breeze
2 Shifting down
3 ESP
4 The song is you
5 Once upon a summertime
[La valse des Lilas]

Astrud Gilberto
That Girl From Ipanema
The Astrud Gilberto Album
The Girl from Ipanema
Astrud Gilberto
Rare Bird CDBID 11001
(D) Jazz Door JD 1222
(D) Flash 8337-2
(GB) Skyline SLCD 818
(GB) That's Jazz TJ 046
(GB) Buda Records 824352
(F) Kardum 650 901

Chet Baker – tp, voc
Astrud Gilberto – voc
James Buffington, Earl Chapin,
John Trevor Clark – frh
Edward Daniels, George Marge,
Raymond Beckenstein, David Tofani – sax
Frank Owens – p
Gene Bertoncini – g
Jay Berliner – g
Ron Carter – b
Rubens Bassini – perc
Ronnie Zito – dr
Mary Eiland, Maureen McElheron,
Joey Dee – backvoc
David Nadien – concertmaster

New York, N.Y. (USA), 1977 (prob)
3 Far away

The Incredible Chet Baker
Plays And Sings
(I) Carosello CDOR 9022
(J) King KICJ-57

Chet Baker – tp, voc on 1, 6
Ruth Young – voc on 1, 6
Bruce Thomas – p
Jacques Pelzer – fl, ss
Gianni Basso – ts
Lucio Terzano – b
Giancarlo Pillot – dr

Milano (I), March 1977
1 Autumn leaves
2 Sad walk
3 Highblown
4 Laura
5 Love vibration
6 Whatever possessed me
7 I waited for you

Torino (I)/Swing Club · March 5, 1977
Gian Carlo Roncaglia

Torino (I)/Swing Club · March 5, 1977
22 *Gian Carlo Roncaglia*

Freddie de Ronde, CB,
Gianni Basso
Macerata (I) · July 22, 1977
Carlo Pieroni

Stan Getz + CB
Macerata (I) · July 22, 1977
Luisa Cairati

Live In Chateauvallon
(F) Esuldon FCD 128

Chet Baker – tp, voc on 4
Phil Markowitz – p
Scott Lee – b
Jeff Brillinger – dr

Chateauvallon (F), Nov 10, 1978
1 House of Jade [Oh you crazy moon]
2 Love for sale
3 Beautiful black eyes
4 There will never be another you
5 Once upon a summertime

Live At Nick's
(NL) Criss Cross CD 1027
(J) Criss Cross 33KN-2032

Chet Baker – tp, voc on 3, 5
Phil Markowitz – p
Scott Lee – b
Jeff Brillinger – dr

Laren (NL), Nov 30, 1978
1 The best thing for you is me
2 Broken wing
3 This is always
4 Beautiful black eyes
5 I remember you
6 Love for sale

Broken Wing
(F) Cornelia Adda 581020
Chet Baker in Paris / Vol. II
(D) West Wind 2059

Chet Baker – tp, voc on 3
Phil Markowitz – p
Jean-François Jenny-Clark – b
Jeff Brillinger – dr

Paris (F), Dec 28, 1978
1 Broken wing
2 [Beautiful] Black eyes
3 Oh, you crazy moon
4 How deep is the ocean
5 Blue Gilles

Two A Day
(F) Dreyfus Jazz Line 191 017-2

Chet Baker – tp, voc on 4
Phil Markowitz – p
Jean-Louis Rassinfosse – b
Jeff Brillinger – dr

Herouville (F), Dec 29, 1978
1 Two a day
2 Blue room
3 If I should lose you
4 This is always
5 The best thing for you is me

Jacques Pelzer + CB
Verviers (B) / Chafati · Nov 1978
Philippe Gielen

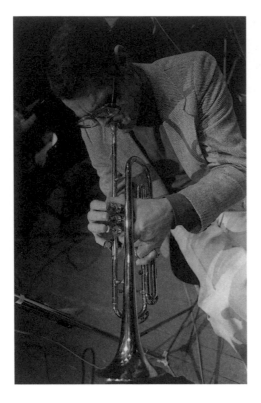

Ludwigsburg (D) / Kulturzentrum
Dec 9, 1978

26 *Hans Kumpf*

CB, Lalle Svensson, Lennart Jansson
Stockholm (S) / Fasching · Dec 11, 1978
Gunnar Holmberg

København (DK)/Montmartre
Dec 12, 1978
Gorm Valentin

København (DK.)/Montmartre
Dec 12, 1978
Jørgen Bo

Phil Markowitz, CB,
Jean-Louis Rassinfosse
Oslo (N)/Club 7 · Dec 14, 1978
Randi Hultin

29

Chet Baker in Europe
(D) b&w bwcd 001

Chet Baker – tp
Wolfgang Lackerschmid – vib

Stuttgart (D), Jan 8, 1979
1 Double-O
2 Why shouldn't you cry (take 2)

Chet Baker &
Wolfgang Lackerschmid
Ballads For Two
(D) INAK 856 CD

Chet Baker – tp
Wolfgang Lackerschmid – vib, perc on 4

Stuttgart (D), Jan 8/9 1979
1 Blue Bossa
2 Five years ago
3 Why shouldn't you cry
4 Dessert
5 Softly as in a morning sunrise
6 You don't know what love is
7 Waltz for Susan

The Touch Of Your Lips
(DK) SteepleChase SCCD-31122
(J) SteepleChase VACE-1007

Chet Baker – tp, voc on 2, 5
Doug Raney – g
Niels-Henning Ørsted Pedersen – b

København (DK), June 21, 1979
1 I waited for you
2 But not for me
3 Autumn in New York
4 Blue room
5 The touch of your lips
6 Star eyes
7 Autumn in New York (take 2)

All Blues
(F) Arco 3 ARC 102
(F) Kardum 645 503

Chet Baker – tp, voc on 11
Rachel Gould – voc
Jean Paul Florens – g on 2
Henry Florens – p
Jim Richardson – b
Tony Mann – dr

London (GB), Sept 4/5, 1979
2 Phil's Bossa
3 I've got you under my skin
7 All Blues
11 Straight, no chaser

Chet Baker – tp, voc on 5, 9
Jean Paul Florens – g
Henry Florens – p on 9
Jim Richardson – b
Tony Mann – dr on 4, 9

London (GB), Sept 4/5, 1979
4 Secret love
5 Round midnight
6 What's new
9 Blues for Inge

Chet Baker – tp
Henry Florens – p
Jim Richardson – b

London (GB), Sept 4/5, 1979
1 My funny Valentine
8 My funny Valentine (take 2)

Chet Baker – tp
Jean Paul Florrens – g

London (GB), Sept 4/5, 1979
12 Round midnight (take 2)
13 Darn that dream

Chet Baker '79
Featuring Rachel Gould
(F) Celluloid CEL 6780

Chet Baker – tp
Rachel Gould – voc
Henry Florens – p
Jim Richardson – b
Tony Mann – dr

London (GB), Sept 4/5, 1979
3 Bangles, bangles and beads

"79" and "All Blues" both feature material
that Chet Baker recorded for the British
Bingow label. The tracks "Secret love",
"My funny Valentine (take 2)" and "Round
midnight (take 2)" are not contained on
"79". "Bangles, Bangles and Beads" appears
on "79" only.

Chet Baker in Europe
(D) b&w bwcd 001

København (DK), Oct 2, 1979
3 Interview with Ib Skovgaard

No Problem
(DK) SteepleChase SCCD-31131

Chet Baker – tp, voc on 7
Duke Jordan – p
Niels-Henning Ørsted Pedersen – b
Norman Fearrington – dr

København (DK), Oct 2, 1979
1 No problem
2 Sultry Eve
3 Glad I met Pat
4 Kiss of Spain
5 The fuzz
6 My queen is home to stay
7 Jealous Blues

Daybreak
(DK) SteepleChase SCCD-31142
(J) SteepleChase VACE-1063
Live at Montmatre/Vol.I
(J) Phonogramm 32JD-10033 CD

Chet Baker – tp, voc on 2
Doug Raney – g
Niels-Henning Ørsted Pedersen – b

København (DK), Oct 4, 1979
1 For minors only
2 Daybreak
3 You can't go home again
4 Broken wing
5 Down

This Is Always
(DK) SteepleChase SCCD-31168
Live At Montmatre/Vol.II
(J) Phonogramm 32JD-10034 CD

Chet Baker – tp, voc on 4
Doug Raney – g
Niels-Henning Ørsted Pedersen – b

København (DK), Oct 4, 1979
1 How deep is the ocean
2 House of Jade
3 Love for sale
4 This is always
5 Way to go out [Lucius Lou]

Someday My Prince Will Come
(DK) SteepleChase SCCD-31180

Chet Baker – tp, voc on 5
Doug Raney – g
Niels-Henning Ørsted Pedersen – b

København (DK), Oct 4, 1979
1 Gnid
2 Love vibrations
3 Sad walk
4 Someday my prince will come
5 I'm old fashioned
6 In your own sweet way

Just Friends
(F) Arco 1180 ARC 112

Chet Baker – tp, voc on 2, 3
Nicola Stilo – fl
Lou D'Ambrosio – p
Peter Dowdall – b
Tony Mann – dr

Zürich (CH), Oct 23, 1979
1 What's new
2 Just friends
3 My foolish heart
4 Strollin'

**Chet Baker/
Wolfgang Lackerschmid
Featuring Larry Coryell,
Buster Williams
And Tony Williams**
(D) INAK 857 CD

Chet Baker – tp, voc on 2
Wolfgang Lackerschmid – vib
Larry Coryell – g
Buster Williams – b
Tony Williams – dr

Stuttgart (D), Nov 1979
1 Mr. Biko
2 Baltzwaltz
3 The latin one
4 Rue Gregoire du Tour
5 Here's that rainy day
6 Toku do

Wolfgang Lackerschmid

I played with Chet over a period of nine years in varying line-ups, mainly smaller tour bands, from the duo up to sextets. He played melodies with such a musical logic that even in the beginning, when I was only twenty-three years old, I could follow him intuitively, although many of his pieces were still unknown to me.

Moreover, he was the only one who interpreted my compositions exactly the way I had imagined them. He hit the right mood and, during recordings, was very concentrated and serious. After the sessions for the duo album, he said to me: "Wolfgang, I'd like to work with you. I like your tunes and your playing and you're a good driver and a good guy to hang out with. So . . . do you want to tour with me?" Of course I was overwhelmed, happy and excited . . .

When we recorded "Why Shouldn't You Cry", the piece did not have a title. I'd only just completed it and had not yet copied out the changes in B♭. I was about to do this when Chet said: "I don't need changes. I got the melody . . .". Of course that says a lot about him and the music itself. If you have the melody you can also master the form and the harmonies, and you don't have to churn out notes according to the dictates of a bunch of harmonic symbols.

After we had recorded the piece our girlfriends and the manager sat in the control room crying. They were so moved by the recording but a little embarassed, too, that we had caught them in such a vulnerable state. Whereupon we both said, "Why shouldn't you cry?", and that became the title.

Mit Chet habe ich über einen Zeitraum von neun Jahren in verschiedensten Besetzungen gespielt, hauptsächlich in seinen kleineren Tourbands, vom Duo bis zum Sextett. Seine Melodien waren musikalisch so logisch, daß ich ihm damals, als Dreiundzwanzigjähriger, intuitiv folgen konnte, obwohl ich viele seiner Stücke noch nicht kannte.

Er war auch der einzige, der meine Kompositionen so interpretierte, wie ich sie mir vorgestellt hatte. Er traf genau die richtige Stimmung und war bei den Aufnahmen sehr konzentriert und ernsthaft bei der Sache. Nach den Sessions für das Duoalbum sagte er zu mir: „Wolfgang, ich möchte mit dir arbeiten. Ich mag deine Stücke und dein Spiel, du bist ein guter Fahrer und jemand, mit dem es sich aushalten läßt. Möchtest du mit mir touren?" Natürlich war ich überwältigt, glücklich und aufgeregt . . .

Als wir „Why Shouldn't You Cry" aufnahmen, hatte das Stück noch keinen Titel. Ich hatte es gerade komponiert und die Changes noch nicht in B♭ ausgeschrieben. Das wollte ich noch schnell machen, aber Chet sagte: „Ich brauch' keine Changes. Ich hab' die Melodie im Kopf . . ." Das sagt natürlich viel über ihn und die Musik an sich aus. Wenn man die Melodie in sich hat, beherrscht man auch die Form und die Harmonien und muß nicht irgendwelche Töne passend zu einem Harmoniesymbol abladen.

Nachdem wir das Stück eingespielt hatten, saßen unsere damaligen Freundinnen und die Managerin im Regieraum und weinten. Die Aufnahme hatte sie so gerührt, aber es war ihnen doch peinlich, daß wir sie so sahen. Darauf sagten wir beide: „Why shouldn't you cry?", und das wurde dann der Titel.

Wolfgang Lackerschmid + CB
Stuttgart (D) / Tonstudio Zuckerfabrik
Jan 8, 1979
Hans Kumpf

Translation: Caroline Mähl

Ruth Young, Michael Kersting,
CB, Rocky Knauer, Michel Graillier,
Jacques Pelzer
Stuttgart (D) / AT-Musikpodium
Jan 16, 1979

34   *Hans Kumpf*

Rocky Knauer

Wie ich Chet kennengelernt habe? Das war eine große Überraschung für mich! Ich erinnere mich, daß ich auf die Uhr sah, als das Telefon klingelte. Es war spät, halb zwei Uhr morgens. Ein Mann mit sanfter Stimme und amerikanischem Westküsten-Akzent fragt mich, ob ich Rocky Knauer sei. Er sagt, er rufe aus Stuttgart an, sein Name sei Chet Baker. Ich hatte gerade Geburtstag gehabt und dachte deshalb zuerst, es wäre ein Freund, der mir einen Streich spielen wollte. Ich sage also: „Ok, wer ist da wirklich?" Der Mann am anderen Ende lacht herzlich, und dann überzeugt er mich recht schnell, daß er tatsächlich Chet Baker ist. Er sagt, er habe Ärger mit seinem Bassisten, ob ich wohl am nächsten Abend mit ihm im AT-Podium spielen könne. Mein Adrenalinspiegel steigt augenblicklich, und mit klopfendem Herzen antworte ich: „Ja, ich habe Zeit und würde sehr gern spielen!" Chet erklärte mir, wo der Club war und in welchem Hotel ich mich einfinden sollte. Da ich zu aufgeregt war, um noch schlafen zu können, legte ich die einzige Chet-Baker-Platte auf, die ich damals besaß, und fing an, die Sachen für den Auftritt zu packen. Was mir als erstes auffiel, war, wie melodiös und lyrisch er spielte und daß er wirklich oft wie Miles klang. Ich konnte es kaum erwarten, zu dem Gig zu kommen!

Abends im Club stellte sich dann heraus, daß der Bassist Jean-Louis Rassinfosse die ersten zwei Stücke spielen sollte, danach war ich an der Reihe. Da ich nicht gerne auf einem fünfsaitigen Baß spiele, würde er sein Instrument von der Bühne nehmen und ich meines mitbringen. Ich empfand die ganze Situation als sehr merkwürdig, fast wie im Zirkus. Es wirkte mehr wie ein Vorspiel vor Publikum als ein richtiger Auftritt. Chet sah zu mir hinüber und sagte: „The Touch Of Your Lips, in B." Während er einzählte, überschlugen sich die Gedanken in meinem Kopf – ich hatte das Stück noch nie gehört. Ich sperrte die Ohren auf und versuchte, so gut es ging, dem Klavier zu folgen. In den zweiten acht Takten verlor ich den Faden, und Chet rief: „Stop, stop! Wir spielen nicht dasselbe!" Mit großem Getöse kam alles zum Stillstand. Mist, ich fühlte mich wie ein Idiot. Ich konnte die Leute förmlich denken hören: „Was für ein Blödmann, geht auf die Bühne und kann nicht spielen." Das mußte es sein, was man so schön als „Lehrgeld bezahlen" bezeichnet. Egal, ich hatte es gerade geschafft, Michel zu fragen, in welcher Tonart die Bridge endet, als ich Chet sagen hörte: „Diesmal aber richtig!". Er zählte das Stück noch einmal ein, nach einem Chorus hatte ich es im Kopf, und danach lief alles bestens.

Would you like to know how I first met Chet? It was a great surprise for me! I remember looking at the clock when the telephone rang. It was late, 1:30 in the morning. A man with a soft voice and a Western American accent asks me if I am Rocky Knauer. He says that he's calling from Stuttgart and that his name is Chet Baker. Since it had just been my birthday, my first thought was that a friend was putting me on, so I say: "Alright, who is this?" I hear a hearty laugh and then the person on the other end of the line quite quickly convinces me that he really is Chet Baker. He says he is having trouble with his bass player and would I have time to play with him tonight at the AT-Podium? My adrenalin immediately rises and while my heart beats faster I answer: "Yes I do have time and would love to play!" He then explained to me where the club is and which hotel to go to. Since I was too excited to sleep I put on the only Chet Baker record that I had at the time and started to pack the things I'd need that evening. The first thing that struck me was how melodiously and lyrically he played, and that he could really sound like Miles. I could hardly wait to get to the gig!

Later in the club it turned out that the bassist Jean-Louis Rassinfosse would play the first couple of tunes and then I would play. Since I felt uncomfortable on a 5-string bass, he'd take his bass off the stage and I'd come up with mine. I felt it was a very strange situation, like being in a circus. More like an audition in front of an audience instead of a gig. Chet looked at me and said, "The Touch Of Your Lips, in B flat." As he counted in the tune, my mind was racing, because I had never heard that tune before. I opened my ears and followed the piano as best as I could. In the middle of the second eight bars I got lost, and Chet shouted real loud, "Stop – stop! We're not playing the same tune!" Everything came to a crashing halt. What a drag. I felt like a fool. I could hear the people thinking, What an idiot, gets on the stage and can't play. That had to be what is called "paying your dues". Well, anyway, I got a chance to ask Michel what key the bridge goes to, when I heard Chet say: "Let's get it together", and counting the tune in again. After one chorus, I had it down and everything was cool.

Übersetzung: Caroline Mähl

Larry Coryell, Hubert Laws, CB,
Ron Carter
Paris (F) · March 8, 1979
36   *Christian Rose*

London (GB) / Roundhouse
March 24, 1979
Jak Kilby

Jean-Louis Rassinfosse, CB, Charlie Rice
London (GB)/Roundhouse
March 24, 1979
Jak Kilby

Phil Markowitz + CB
London (GB)/Roundhouse
March 24, 1979
Jak Kilby

London (GB)/Roundhouse
March 24, 1979
Jak Kilby

Genève (CH)/New Morning · June 1979
Dany Gignoux

Genève (CH) / New Morning
June 13, 1979
Dany Gignoux

Michel Graillier, CB,
Jean-Louis Rassinfosse
Kongsberg (N) · June 29, 1979
Randi Hultin   **43**

◀ Pavia (I)/Centro Civico Mirabello
Sept 14, 1979
Paolo Ferraresi

Pavia (I)/Centro Civico Mirabello
Sept 14, 1979
Carlo Verri   **45**

The first time I met Chet Baker was
outside Sweet Silence studios in Copenhagen, where we were to record the "The
Touch Of Your Lips" date. The engineer-
owner of the studio hadn't shown up yet so
we sat outside waiting for him to arrive.
Chet struck me as a rather quiet person, at
any rate he didn't say much. When the
session finally got started he asked, "What
do you want to play?", which surprised me.
He did have some music with him, though.
I remember suggesting "Autumn In New
York". I think he chose the rest of the
tunes. Chet was having trouble with his
chops although it turned out to be a pretty
good session.

He called me about a month later and
asked if I would come to Paris and play
with him. We did two weeks at the Club
St-Germain. The first few days were pretty
much like the record date as far as Chet
was concerned. Then suddenly one night
his chops were fine and he played like a
whirlwind, fast long lines with that perfect
timing he had. It scared me a bit. I remember thinking, This guy's a giant!

I continued working with him for a few
months, mostly one-nighters in France,
Switzerland, Belgium, Germany, Holland,
Italy, and finally Copenhagen where we did
the live records at the "Montmartre". After
that session I played a few more gigs with
him in Germany but there was a mixup, he
sent me to the wrong town, so after
spending the whole day looking for a
non-existent jazz concert I gave up and
went home. I called him a few days later
and explained what had happened but I
had the feeling that he didn't believe me,
that he thought I was tired of touring
(which I was) and had gone home for that
reason.

46   Photo: Paolo Ferraresi

Doug Raney

Das erste Mal traf ich Chet Baker vor den Sweet Silence Studios in
Kopenhagen, wo wir „The Touch Of Your Lips" aufnehmen sollten. Der
Toningenieur, gleichzeitig Besitzer des Studios, war noch nicht erschie-
nen, und wir saßen draußen, um auf ihn zu warten. Chet schien mir ein
eher stiller Mensch zu sein, jedenfalls sagte er nicht viel. Als es dann
endlich losging, fragte er zu meiner Überraschung: „Was willst du
spielen?". Er hatte allerdings auch selbst Musik dabei. Ich erinnere mich,
daß ich „Autumn In New York" vorschlug. Ich glaube, die restlichen
Stücke wählte er aus. Obwohl Chet nicht ganz fit war, wurde es doch eine
recht gute Session.

Etwa einen Monat später rief er mich an und fragte, ob ich mit ihm
in Paris spielen wolle. Wir traten zwei Wochen lang im Club St-Germain
auf. Die ersten paar Abende ähnelten mehr oder weniger den Studioaufnahmen, was Chet betraf, aber dann, eines Nachts, war er in
Höchstform und spielte wie ein Wirbelwind, schnelle, lange Linien mit
dem für ihn typischen perfekten Timing. Er machte mir fast ein bißchen
Angst. Ich weiß, daß ich dachte: „Dieser Typ ist unglaublich!"

Ich arbeitete noch einige Monate weiter mit ihm, meist bei einzelnen
Auftritten in Frankreich, der Schweiz, Belgien, Deutschland, Holland,
Italien und schließlich in Kopenhagen, wo wir die Live-Alben im
„Montmartre" aufnahmen. Nach dieser Session spielten wir noch ein
paar Konzerte in Deutschland, aber zum Schluß kam es zu einem
Mißverständnis, er schickte mich in die falsche Stadt, und nachdem ich
einen geschlagenen Tag nach einem nicht existierenden Jazzkonzert
gesucht hatte, gab ich auf und fuhr nach Hause. Ich rief ihn ein paar
Tage später an und erklärte die Geschichte, hatte aber das Gefühl, daß
er mir nicht glaubte. Er schien zu denken, ich hätte das Herumreisen
satt (was auch stimmte) und wäre aus diesem Grund nach Hause
gefahren.

Ich spielte gern mit ihm, aber mit Chet unterwegs zu sein, war nicht
gerade ein Zuckerschlecken. Es gab ständig Mißverständnisse und
Probleme. Weil ich wußte, daß er immer Drogen dabei hatte – sein
Kofferraum war voll mit Pillen und anderem Zeug –, reiste ich schließlich

Doug Raney
Pavia (I)/Centro Civico Mirabello
Sept 14, 1979
Paolo Ferraresi   **47**

Although I enjoyed playing with him, the tours were by no means picnics. There were always mixups, practical problems, etc. I ended up travelling by myself because I knew he had drugs. The trunk of his car was filled with all kinds of pills and stuff. After one incident at the Swiss border, I insisted on crossing borders without him.

I remember the day I arrived in Paris. It was a Wednesday. He had called me about a week before and had said that the first gig would be on a Thursday. I didn't think about it when he asked me to come on Wednesday, I thought he just wanted to rehearse or something. A few hours after I arrived, we drove to Barney Wilen's house in Monte Carlo in Chet's Citroën CX which he drove like a race car maniac. We had a gig just over the border in Italy. When we arrived at Barney's house he started talking about going to the gig. I mentioned that I thought the gig was on the next day, which produced a blank look on Chet's face followed by, "Oh yeah, you're right, why didn't you say something in Paris?".

The gig in Italy was weird, like a scene from a Fellini film. There were all kinds of people hanging on to the scaffolding above us (it was an outdoor concert). Also, there was a guy sitting on a chair on the stage with a beer in his hand throughout the concert. When we were finished, he got up, bowed to the audience, and collapsed.

We were always getting invited to some prominent person's home after we played. Chet was kind of a cult figure, especially in Italy where he had been in jail. He had wealthy friends in most European countries where he could stay for a few weeks or even months.

Another funny incident occurred in Italy. We were at the airport, and there were problems with the bass. We had a ticket for it but they wouldn't let us take it on the plane. Finally they asked the captain who has the final say in such matters. He approached us and suddenly burst out: "Chet Baker! I have all of your records!" Needless to say, we were allowed to take the bass along. We were given champagne, Chet signed autographs, and we were invited to the cockpit. I thought they were going to let Chet fly the plane.

After that tour I didn't see Chet for a couple of years. Then one day while in Stockholm I received a call to do a concert with him. I think it was in Örebro. Chet played the drums. A few years later, in '85 or '86, I did a couple of concerts with him in Copenhagen and Amsterdam. That was the last time I played with him.

allein, und nach einem Zwischenfall an der Schweizer Grenze bestand ich darauf, grundsätzlich ohne ihn über die Grenze zu gehen.

Ich kann mich noch gut an den Tag erinnern, an dem ich in Paris ankam. Es war ein Mittwoch. Chet hatte mich ungefähr eine Woche zuvor angerufen und mir mitgeteilt, das erste Konzert finde am Donnerstag statt. Ich dachte mir nichts dabei, als er sagte, ich solle am Mittwoch anreisen; ich nahm an, er wollte proben oder so etwas. Ein paar Stunden nach meiner Ankunft fuhren wir in Chets Citroën CX (er hatte einen Fahrstil wie ein durchgedrehter Rennfahrer) zu Barney Wilens Haus in Monte Carlo. Wir hatten einen Gig in Italien, gleich jenseits der Grenze. Als wir bei Barney ankamen, meinte Chet, wir sollten sofort rüberfahren. Als ich erwiderte, meiner Meinung nach sei das Konzert erst am nächsten Tag, sah er mich mit leerem Blick an und sagte dann: „Ach ja, richtig, warum hast du das nicht schon in Paris gesagt?"

Das Konzert in Italien war seltsam, wie ein Ausschnitt aus einem Fellini-Film. Es fand draußen statt, und in den Gerüsten über uns hingen Trauben von Menschen. Außerdem saß während des gesamten Konzerts ein Typ auf der Bühne, auf einem Stuhl und mit einem Bier in der Hand. Als wir fertig waren, stand er auf, verbeugte sich zum Publikum und kippte um.

Nach den Konzerten wurden wir immer in die Häuser irgendwelcher prominenter Leute eingeladen. Chet war so eine Art Kultfigur, besonders in Italien, wo er im Gefängnis gesessen hatte. Er hatte in fast allen Ländern Europas reiche Freunde, bei denen er ein paar Wochen oder sogar Monate bleiben konnte.

In Italien passierte noch etwas Komisches. Wir waren am Flughafen, und es gab Probleme mit dem Baß. Wir hatten ein Ticket für das Instrument, aber sie wollten es uns trotzdem nicht mit ins Flugzeug nehmen lassen. Schließlich wurde der Flugkapitän konsultiert, der in solchen Angelegenheiten das letzte Wort hat. Er kam auf uns zu und platzte plötzlich heraus: „Chet Baker! Ich habe all Ihre Platten!" Danach durften wir den Baß natürlich mitnehmen. Man servierte uns Champagner, Chet schrieb Autogramme, und wir wurden ins Cockpit eingeladen. Ich dachte schon, sie würden Chet auch noch das Flugzeug fliegen lassen.

Nach dieser Tour sah ich Chet zwei Jahre lang nicht. Dann erhielt ich eines Tages einen Anruf in Stockholm, ob ich Zeit für ein Konzert hätte. Ich glaube, es war in Örebro, und Chet spielte Schlagzeug. Einige Jahre später, 1985 oder 86, hatten wir ein paar Gigs in Kopenhagen und Amsterdam. Das war das letzte Mal, daß ich mit ihm spielte.

Übersetzung: Caroline Mähl

Pavia (I)/Centro Civico Mirabello
Sept 14, 1979
Paolo Ferraresi

CB + Ruth Young
København (DK)/Plaza Hotel
Oct 2, 1979

50 *Gorm Valentin*

København (DK)/Plaza Hotel
Oct 2, 1979

Gorm Valentin

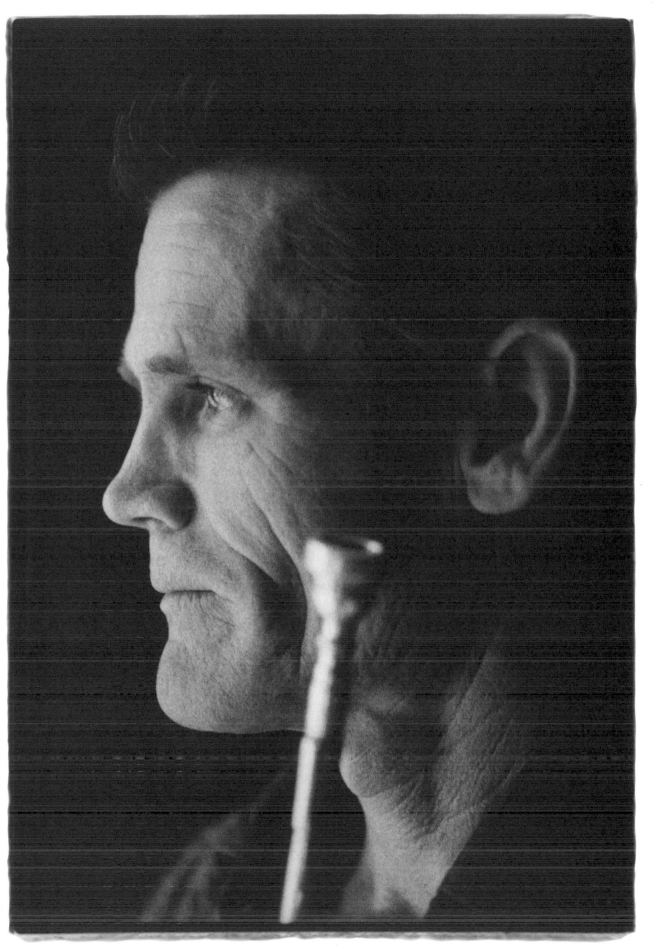

Niels-Henning Ørsted Pedersen

I don't think Chet ever got the respect he really deserved. At times in his life he must have felt that he was overlooked. To me he was one of the most melodic players, one of the most sensitive players . . . very adventurous and imaginative . . . any superlative I can come up with belongs to him. At the same time, of course, I am fully aware of the fact that he disappointed a lot of people: because his lifestyle was different from that of the so-called average man. But in retrospect I think what stands out is his immense maturity as a melodic player and his contribution to the art form of jazz – which is the art of the individual. As time goes by and you look back at what happened in the Fifties, Sixties, and Seventies, Chet Baker stands out as one of the major artists of the era.

Ich glaube, man hat Chet nie den Respekt entgegengebracht, den er wirklich verdiente. Es muß Zeiten gegeben haben, in denen er sich übergangen fühlte. Für mich war er einer der melodischsten und sensibelsten Spieler überhaupt, ungemein risikofreudig und einfallsreich – jeder Superlativ, der mir einfällt, paßt auf ihn. Natürlich bin ich mir auch bewußt, daß er viele Menschen enttäuscht hat, weil sein Lebensstil so ganz anders war als der des sogenannten Durchschnittsbürgers. Trotzdem glaube ich, was letztlich am meisten Gewicht hat, ist seine ungeheure spielerische Reife und sein Beitrag zum Jazz, einer Kunstform, die schließlich von Individualität geprägt ist. Wenn man heute zurückblickt auf das, was in den fünfziger, sechziger und siebziger Jahren passierte, dann wird deutlich, daß Chet Baker einer der wichtigsten Künstler jener Zeit war.

CB + Niels-Henning Ørsted Pedersen
København (DK)/Montmartre
Oct 4, 1979
Jørgen Bo

Übersetzung: Caroline Mähl

Hamburg (D)/Fabrik · Oct 20, 1979
Ralph Quinke

CB, Jean-Louis Rassinfosse,
Louis McConnell
Milano (I)/Cinema Teatro Anteo
Nov 19, 1979

54 *Carlo Verri*

Enrico Pieranunzi + CB
Roma (I) · Dec 4, 1979
Fabrizio Biamonte

Enrico Pieranunzi*

Wenn Chet beschloß, daß ein bestimmtes Stück gespielt werden sollte, dann deshalb, weil er in dem Augenblick gerade dieses Stück brauchte, um sich auszudrücken. Für ihn war jedes Stück wie ein lebendiges Wesen, mit dem er immer wieder aufs neue Bekanntschaft schloß und dessen Gesicht, ob lächelnd oder weinend, er jedesmal neu entdeckte. Er kannte die Texte zu fast allen Titeln, die wir spielten, die Geschichten, die darin erzählt wurden, und diese Geschichten erweckte er zu neuem Leben.

Ich erinnere mich an mein Erstaunen, als wir „Soft Journey" für Edi-Pan aufnahmen. Ich hatte unser Notenmaterial sorgfältig vorbereitet: Melodie, Harmonien, alles. Er sagte mir: „Nein, die Harmonien interessieren mich nicht, spiel' das Stück einige Male, ich werde es lernen."
Sein musikalisches Gehör war außergewöhnlich, ebenso wie seine Fähigkeit, das Publikum zu zwingen, dem zuzuhören, was seine Trompete und seine Stimme zu erzählen hatten.

When Chet decided that we should play a particular piece it was because at that moment he needed exactly that piece to express himself. For him each piece was a living thing he would return to again and again and whose features, whether happy or sad, he rediscovered every time. He knew the lyrics to almost all the titles we played, the stories they contained, and in his performances he revived those stories.

I remember how amazed I was when we recorded "Soft Journey" for Edi-Pan. I had prepared our material painstakingly: melody, harmonies, everything. He told me: "No, I'm not interested in the harmonies, play the piece a few times, I'm going to learn it." His ear was extraordinary, as was his ability to force the audience into listening to what his trumpet and his voice had to say.

Übersetzung: Giuseppe de Siati
*aus „Musica Jazz", Juli 1988

Translation: Caroline Mähl
*from "Musica Jazz", July 1988

Seven Faces Of Valentine
(I) Philology W 30-2

Chet Baker – tp, voc
Enrico Pieranunzi – p

Roma (I), Jan 4, 1980
2 My funny Valentine

Burnin' At Backstreet
(E) Fresh Sound Records FSR-CD 128

Chet Baker – tp, voc on 6
Drew Salperto – p
Mike Formanek – b
Art Frank – dr

New Haven, Conn. (USA), Feb 19, 1980
1 *Tune up*
2 *Milestones*
3 *Blue 'n' Boogie*
4 *Stella by starlight*
5 *Four* (it)
6 *Just friends* (it)

Chet Baker – Steve Houben
(F) 52e Rue Est RECD 019

Chet Baker – tp, voc on 1, 4
Steve Houben – as/out on 1
Bill Frisell – g
Dennis Luxion – p
Kermit Driscoll – b
Bruno Castellucci – dr

Bruxelles (B), Feb 1980
1 This is always
2 Sweet Martine
3 Beatrice
4 Deep in a dream

Ron Carter & Chet Baker
Patrão
(I) Milestone MCD-9099-2

Chet Baker – tp
Ron Carter – b
Kenny Barron – p
Jack DeJohnette – dr

Englewood Cliffs, N.J. (USA)
May 19/20, 1980
1 *Tail feathers*
2 *Yours truly*
4 *Nearly*
6 *Yours truly (One more time)*

Chet Baker – tp
Ron Carter – b
Kenny Barron – p-solo
Aloisio Aguiar – p
Amaury Tristao – g
Edison Machado – dr
Nana Vasconcelos – perc

3 *Ah, Rio*
5 *Third plane*

Night Bird
(D) West Wind CD 2038

Chet Baker – tp
Karl Ratzer – g
Nicola Stilo – fl
Riccardo Del Fra – b
Al Levitt – dr

Paris (F), June 25, 1980
1 Leaving
2 D.S. Dilemma
3 Night bird
4 Tempus fugit
5 Tune up

Tune Up
(D) West Wind CD 2037

Chet Baker – tp, voc on 3
Karl Ratzer – g
Nicola Stilo – fl
Riccardo Del Fra – b
Al Levitt – dr/out on 2

Paris (F), June 25/27, 1980
1 Tune up
2 No ties
3 There will never be another you

Chet Baker &
The Boto Brasilian Quartet
(F) Dreyfus Jazz Line 849 228-2

Chet Baker – tp, voc on 3, 5
Richard Galliano – acc
Rique Pantoja Leite – p
Michel Peyratoux – b
José Boto – dr, perc

Paris (F), July 21-23, 1980
1 Salsamba
2 Balsa
3 Forgetful
4 Inaïa
5 Seila
6 Balao
7 Julinho

Roma (I) · Jan 4, 1980
Fabrizio Biamonte

Mannheim (D) / Capitol · Nov 13, 1980
Manfred Rinderspacher

Larry Coryell + CB
Mannheim (D)/Capitol · Nov 13, 1980
58 *Manfred Rinderspacher*

Larry Coryell + CB
Genève (CH)/New Morning
Nov 15, 1980
Dany Gignoux

Genève (CH)/New Morning
Nov 15, 1980
Dany Gignoux

59

Live At Fat Tuesday's
(E) Fresh Sound Records FSR-CD 131

Chet Baker – tp, voc on 4
Bud Shank – as on 2, 3, 4
Phil Markowitz – p on 1
Hal Galper – p on 2, 3, 4
Ron Carter – b
Ben Riley – dr

New York, N.Y. (USA), April 28, 1981
1 You can't go home again
2 Ray's idea
3 In your own sweet way
4 There will never be another you

Chet Baker
(F) Carlyne CARCD 15
(J) DIW-339

Chet Baker – tp, voc on 3, 5, 6
René Urtreger – p
Pierre Michelot – b
Aldo Romano – dr

Paris (F), Nov 3, 1981
1 For minors only
2 Chasing the Bird
3 But not for me
4 Down
5 My funny Valentine
6 Just friends

Michel Graillier
Dream Drops
(F) Owl 026 CD 3800262

Chet Baker – tp
Michel Graillier – p

Paris (F), Nov 13, 1981
5 Dream drops

Ludwigshafen (D) · March 12, 1981
Manfred Rinderspacher

Jean-François Jenny-Clark,
CB, Philip Catherine
Ludwigshafen (D) · March 12, 1981

62 *Manfred Rinderspacher*

Sal Nistico + CB
London (GB)/Roundhouse
March 20, 1981

Jak Kilby

Hamburg (D)
Hotel an der Alster / Bellevue · 1981
64   *Ralph Quinke*

Colombes (F) · May 1981
Thierry Nectoux

Peace
(D) Enja 4016-04
(USA) Rhino R21Y-79625
(J) Enja K30Y-6233
(J) Enja ENJ-1021

Chet Baker – tp
Dave Friedman – mar, vib
Buster Williams – b
Joe Chambers – dr

New York, N.Y. (USA), Feb 23, 1982
1 Syzygies [3+1=5]
2 Peace
3 Lament for Thelonious
4 The song is you
5 Shadows
6 For now
7 3+1=5 (at)

Jim Hall
Youkali
(D) CTI 1001-2
(USA) CTI R2-79480
(J) Phonogram POCJ-1109

Jim Hall – g
Chet Baker – tp
+ various musicians overdubbed

Englewood Cliffs, N.J. (USA)
March/April 1982 (overdubbed in 1992)
2 Django
4 All Blues

Sir Roland Hanna – p
Chet Baker – tp
+ various musicians overdubbed

Englewood Cliffs, N.J. (USA)
June/July 1982 (overdubbed in 1992)
3 Skylark

Out Of Nowhere
(USA) Milestone MCD 9191-2
(J) Milestone VICJ-108

Chet Baker – tp, voc on 2
Frank Adams – as, fl
Frank Brown – g
Ted Adams – b on 1, 2, 6
Ron Adams – eb on 3-5, 7, 8
Wade Robertson – dr

Tulsa, Okla. (USA), Dec 24, 1982
1 Fine and Dandy
2 There will never be another you
3 Lady be good
4 Au privave
5 All the things you are
6 Out of nowhere
7 There is no greater love
8 The Theme

Roma (I) · Jan 1982
Marcello Mencarini

Seven Faces Of Valentine
(I) Philology W 30-2

Chet Baker – tp, voc
Stan Getz – ts
Gil Goldstein – p
George Mraz – p
Victor Lewis – dr

København (DK), Feb 15, 1983
6 My funny Valentine

Stan Getz & Chet Baker
Line For Lyons
(F) Vogue 651 600034
(F) Sonet 30367
(GB) Sonet SNTCD-899
(USA) Gazell CD 1006
(J) Polydor J33J-20116
(J) Sonet ALCB-71

Chet Baker – tp, voc on 1, 4
Stan Getz – ts
Jim McNeely – p
George Mraz – b
Victor Lewis – dr

Stockholm (S), Feb 18, 1983
1 Just friends
2 Stella by starlight
3 Airegin
4 My funny Valentine
5 Milestones
6 Dear old Stockholm
7 Line for Lyons

Seven Faces Of Valentine
(I) Philology W 30-2

Chet Baker – tp, voc
Michel Graillier – p

Angoulême (F), March 5, 1983
4 My funny Valentine

Mister B
(NL) Timeless CDSJP 192

Chet Baker – tp, voc on 8
Kirk Lightsey – p
Eddie Gladden – dr
David Eubanks – b

Monster (NL), March 14, 1983
7 Ray's idea
8 Everything happens to me

Chet Baker – tp
Michel Graillier – p
Riccardo Del Fra – b

Monster (NL), May 25, 1983
1 Dolphin dance
2 Ellen and David
3 Strollin'
4 In your own sweet way
5 Mister B
6 Beatrice

Tracks 1-6 and 8 also released as
Everything Happens To Me
(J) Timeless Alfa 30R2-6

Tracks 7 and 8 appear also on
Kirk Lightsey & Chet Baker
Everything Happens To Me
(NL) Timeless CDSJ 176

Tracks 1 and 8 also released as CD single
Everything Happens To Me
(J) Timeless Alfa 10R3-5
(J) Timeless Alfa ALCR-247

Track 8 also appears on a revised version,
with one bonus track, of
Chet Baker Sings Again
(NL) Timeless CDSJP 238

Naima (The Unusual Chet/Vol. 1)
(I) Philology W 52-2

Stockholm (S), June 4, 1983
Chet Baker – tp, voc
Hank Jones – p
Red Mitchell – b
Shelly Manne – dr

Stockholm (S), June 4, 1983
1 Chet's Blues

Elvis Costello
Punch The Clock
(GB) RCA/F-Beat ZD 70026
(GB) Demon Fiend CD 72
(USA) Columbia CK 38897
(J) RCA R32P-1031

Chet Baker – tp
Elvis Costello – voc
Steve Nieve – p
Bruce Thomas – eb
Pete Thomas – dr
David Bedford – string arr

London (GB), Summer 1983
6 Shipbuilding

Also on
The Best Of Elvis Costello
(Compilation)
(GB) Demon CD FI 52
(USA) Columbia CK 40101
Girls! Girls! Girls! (Compilation)
(GB) Demon Fiend CD 160
(USA) Columbia C2K 46897

A Trumpet For The Sky
Club 21, Paris
Vol. 1
(I) Philology W 55.2
Vol. 2
(I) Philology W 56.2

Chet Baker – tp, voc on 3, 8, 15
Michael Graillier – p
Riccardo Del Fra – b

Paris (F), Sept 1983
1 Leaving
2 Margerine
3 My funny Valentine
4 Love for sale (it)
5 Funk in deep freeze (it)
6 Ellen and David
7 Arbor way
8 Just friends (it)
9 Margerine

10 Cheryl
11 When I fall in love
12 Mr. B
13 Sad walk
14 Four
15 This is always
16 Arbor way

Baker/
Catherine/Rassinfosse
Strollin'
(B) Igloo IGL 034
(CDN) Amplitude JACD-4003

Chet Baker – tp
Philip Catherine – g
Jean-Louis Rassinfosse – b

Bruxelles (B), Sept 1983
1 Crystal bells
2 Strollin'
3 Lament
4 Leaving
5 Cherokee
6 Estate

Chet Baker with Åke Johansson Trio
Live In Sweden
(S) Dragon DRCD 178

Chet Baker – tp, voc on 2, 8
Åke Johansson – p
Kjell Jansson – b
Göran Levin – dr

Göteborg (S), Sept 29, 1983
1 Lament
2 My ideal
3 Beatrice
4 Ellen David
5 You can't go home again
6 Ray's idea
7 Milestones
8 But not for me

At Capolinea
(I) Red Records CD 123206

Chet Baker – tp
Nicola Stilo – fl
Diane Vavra – ss on 2
Michel Graillier – p
Riccardo Del Fra – b
Leo Mitchell – dr

Milano (I), October 1983
1 Estate
2 Francamente
3 Dream drop
4 Lament
5 Pioggia sul Deserto
6 Finestra sul Mare

Live At New Morning
(J) Century/Marshmallow CECC 00420

Chet Baker – tp, voc on 2, 3
Duke Jordan – p
Jesper Lundgaard – b
Leo Mitchell – dr

Paris (F), Nov 24, 1983
1 Out of nowhere
2 My funny Valentine
3 I remember you
4 New Morning Blues (it)

September Song
(J) Century/Marshmallow CECC 00216

Chet Baker – tp, voc on 1-4
Duke Jordan – p
Jesper Lundgaard – b

Paris (F), Nov 24, 1983
1 September song
2 My funny Valentine
3 I remember you
4 But beautiful
6 September song
7 Solar

Lauwe (B), Nov 25, 1983
5 Barbados

Star Eyes
(J) Century/Marshmallow CECC 00206

Chet Baker – tp
Duke Jordan – p
Jesper Lundgaard – b

Arnhem (NL), Nov 28, 1983
1 Walkin'
2 Solar
3 Star eyes

George Mraz, Stan Getz, CB
København (DK)/Montmarte
Feb 15, 1983
Jørgen Bo

Alby Cullaz, Michel Graillier, CB
Paris (F)/New Morning
March 10, 1983
70 *Christian Rose*

København (DK)/Montmartre
May 10, 1983
John R. Johnsen   **71**

Red Mitchell, Hank Jones, CB
Stockholm (S)/Skeppsholmen
June 4, 1983

Gunnar Holmberg

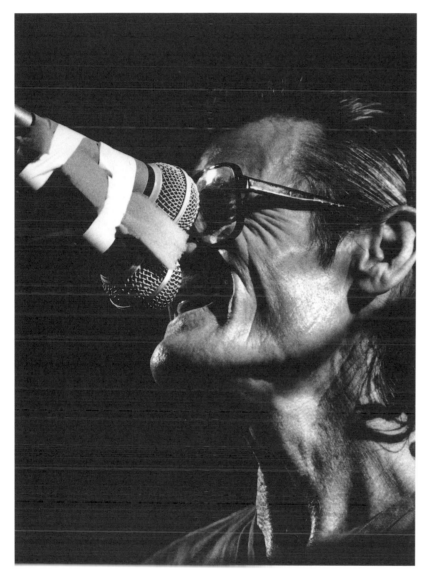

Santander (E) · July 29, 1983
Federico Gonzáles

Tete Montoliu + CB
Santander (E) · July 29, 1983
Federico Gonzáles

Randi Hultin

I first met Chet Baker in Paris at the "Chat Qui Pêche" back in 1963. I remember his trumpet was stolen during the intermission, and he borrowed another one from Hans Kennel, a Swiss musician. I did not understand at that time how he could possibly lose his horn so quickly but I found out after a while that he quite often showed up at gigs without a trumpet. He always had his mouthpiece with him, though, and was always willing to give the audience his best.

When I met Chet next time in 1978 at the "Club 7" in Oslo he told me that he had used Kennel's trumpet for seven years. We became good friends, and he also stayed in my house together with Diane. I loved to listen to his playing but, tender and sorrowful as he often looked, I felt almost guilty when I was listening. He gave so much, and I felt that we were stealing all the power from him.

Das erste Mal begegnete ich Chet Baker 1963 in Paris, im „Chat Qui Pêche". Ich erinnere mich, daß ihm während der Pause die Trompete gestohlen wurde und er sich von Hans Kennel, einem Schweizer Musiker, ein anderes Instrument leihen mußte. Damals verstand ich nicht, wie man sein Horn so schnell verlieren kann, aber mit der Zeit fand ich heraus, daß er ziemlich oft ohne Trompete zu Konzerten kam. Sein Mundstück hatte er allerdings immer dabei, und er war auch immer bereit, auf der Bühne sein Bestes zu geben.

Als ich Chet das nächste Mal traf, 1978 im „Club 7" in Oslo, erzählte er mir, daß er Kennels Trompete sieben Jahre lang gespielt hatte. Wir wurden gute Freunde, und er und Diane wohnten eine Zeitlang bei uns. Ich liebte es, seinem Spiel zuzuhören, aber weil er oft so müde und traurig aussah, hatte ich dabei fast ein schlechtes Gewissen. Er gab soviel, und ich hatte das Gefühl, als würden wir ihm all seine Kraft rauben.

CB + Randi Hultin
Oslo (N) · Aug 1983
74 Archive R.H.

Übersetzung: Caroline Mähl

Göteborg (S) · Sept 1983
Dan Kjellman

Kjell Jansson + CB
Göteborg (S)/Nefertiti · Sept 29, 1983
Gunnar Holmberg

CB + Jacques Pelzer
Liège (B)/Théâtre de la Place · Nov 1983
Philippe Gielen

Paris (F)/New Morning
Nov 23, 1983
Philippe Cibille

Diane Vavra, Maurice Cullaz,
Liliane Rovére, CB
Paris (F) / New Morning · Nov 23, 1983
78   *Philippe Cibille*

CB + Duke Jordan
Paris (F)/New Morning · Nov 24, 1983
Christian Rose

Chet Baker Plays Vladimir Cosma
(F) Carrere 96.251

Chet Baker – tp, voc on 1
Maurice Vander – p
Herve Sellin – p on 7
Niels-Henning Ørsted Pedersen – b
John Guerin – dr
Pierre Gossez – cl, bcl, as on 1, 3, 5, 7, 8
Paul Minck – oboe on 5
Jean-Jacques Justafre – oboe on 1, 7

Paris (F), Sept 1984
1 B.B. Blues
2 Yves et Danielle
3 Hobbylog
4 Promenade sentimentale
5 12+12 [Le Jumeau]
6 Two much
7 Douceurs Ternaires
8 Pintade a jeun

Chet Baker Featuring Warne Marsh
Blues For A Reason
(NL) Criss Cross 1010 CD
(J) Criss Cross 33KN-2030

Chet Baker – tp
Warne Marsh – ts
Hod O'Brian – p
Cecil McBee – b
Eddie Gladden – dr

Monster (NL), Sept 30, 1984
1 Well spoken
2 If you could see me now
3 We know it's love
4 Looking good tonight
5 Imagination
6 Blues for a reason
7 Looking good tonight (take 2)
8 We know it's love (take 2)

Live At Buffalo
(USA) CCB Productions CCB/CD CD 1223

Chet Baker – tp, voc on 2
Sal Nistico – ts
Lorne Lofsky – g
Chris Conners – b
Art Frank – dr

Buffalo, N.Y. (USA), Nov 11, 1984
1 *Stella by starlight*
2 *I remember you*
3 *Night bird*
4 *I'm old fashioned*
5 *Margerine*

Rique Pantoja E Chet Baker
(BR) WEA 255155-2
(USA) Tropical Storm/
WEA Latina WH 55155
(J) Canyon D22Y-0342

Chet Baker – tp
Rique Pantoja – keyb
Marco Fratini – b
Roberto Gatto – dr
Michele Ascolese – g
Stefane Rossini – perc

Roma (I), 1984
3 Arbor way

Diane Vavra + CB
Västerås (S) · April 15, 1984
Gunnar Holmberg

Kjell Jansson, CB, Åke Johansson
Västerås (S) · April 15, 1984
82   *Gunnar Holmberg*

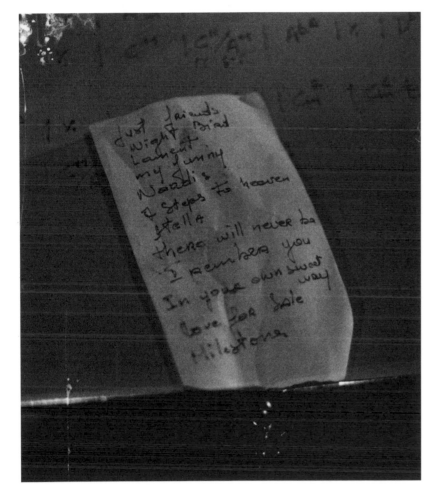

Strasbourg (F) / Lazy Bird · June 1984
Bernd Bingler

83

My Foolish Heart
(I) IRD TDM 002-2

Chet Baker – tp, voc on 2, 6
Martha Burks – voc on 1, 3
Fred Raulston – vib on 1, 3
Floyd Darling – p
Kirby Steward – b
Paul Guerrero – dr

Dallas, Tex. (USA), Jan 13/14, 1985
1 Girl talk
2 My foolish heart
3 The lady is a tramp
4 Solar
5 My funny Valentine
6 But not for me

Misty
(I) IRD TDM 003-2

Chet Baker – tp, voc on 1, 2
Martha Burks – voc on 3, 6
Fred Raulston – vib on 3, 5
Floyd Darling – p
Kirby Steward – b
Paul Guerrero – dr

Dallas, Tex. (USA), Jan 13/14, 1985
1 When I fall in love
2 There will never be another you
3 Misty
4 Mr. B
5 I love my wife
6 Time after time

Time After Time
(I) IRD TDM 004-2

Chet Baker – tp
Martha Burks – voc on 1-4
Fred Raulston – vib on 1-4
Floyd Darling – p
Kirby Steward – b
Paul Guerrero – dr

Dallas, Tex. (USA), Jan 13/14, 1985
1 Like someone in love
2 Time after time
3 The lady is a tramp
4 Almost like being in love
5 My foolish heart
6 Chet swings [Mr. B]

Chet Baker & Paul Bley
Diane
(DK) SteepleChase SCCD-31207
(J) Phonogramm 32JD-10130
(J) SteepleChase VACE-1008

Chet Baker – tp, voc on 2
Paul Bley – p

København (DK), Feb 27, 1985
1 If I should lose you
2 You go to my head
3 How deep is the ocean
4 Pent-up house
5 Everytime we say goodbye
6 Diane
7 Skidadidlin'
8 Little girl blue

Chet Baker in Europe
(D) b&w bwcd 001

København (DK), March 1, 1985
4 Interview with Ib Skovgaard

Seven Faces Of Valentine
(I) Philology W 30-2

Chet Baker – tp, voc
Philip Catherine – g
Jean-Louis Rassinfosse – b

Bologna (I), April 1985
1 My funny Valentine

Chet's Choice
(NL) Criss Cross 1016 CD
(J) Criss Cross 33KN-2031

Chet Baker – tp
Philip Catherine – g
Hein Van de Geyn – b

Monster (NL), June 6, 1985
8 Adriano
9 Blues in the closet
10 Stella by starlight

Chet Baker – tp, voc on 5
Philip Catherine – g
Jean-Louis Rassinfosse – b

Monster (NL), June 25, 1985
1 If I should lose you
2 Sad walk
3 How deep is the ocean
4 Doodlin'
5 My foolish heart
6 Conception
7 Love for sale

Strollin'
(D) Enja CD 5005-11
(USA) Rhino R21Y-79626
(J) Enja ENJ-1013

Chet Baker – tp, voc on 5
Philip Catherine – g
Jean-Louis Rassinfosse – b

Münster (D), June 21, 1985
1 Sad walk
2 Strollin'
3 Love for sale
4 Leaving
5 But not for me

Candy
(GB) Sonet SNTCD-946
(F) Sonet 30359
(USA) Gazell CD 1001
(J) Sonet ALCB-79

Chet Baker – tp, voc on 3
Jean-Louis Rassinfosse – b
Michel Graillier – p

Lidingö/Stockholm (S), June 30, 1985
1 Love for sale
2 Nardis
3 Candy
4 Bye bye Blackbird
5 Sad walk
6 Tempus fugit
7 Red's Blues

Ghiglione/Melillo/Baker
Goodbye, Chet
(I) Philology W 22-2

Chet Baker – tp
Mike Melillo – p
Massimo Moriconi – b
Giampaolo Ascolese dr
+ Orchestra Filarmonica Marchigiani

Macerata (I), July 2, 1985
11 If you could see me now

Mike Melillo & Chet Baker
Symphonically
(I) Soul Note SN 1134 CD

Chet Baker – tp, voc on 4
Mike Melillo – p
Massimo Moriconi – b
Giampaolo Ascolese – dr
+ Orchestra Filarmonica Marchigiani

Macerata (I), July 8, 1985
1 Laura
2 This thing by starlight
3 Yesterdays
4 My foolish heart
5 Dancing in the dark

Jean-Jacques Goldman
Non Homologué
(F) CBS CD 26678
(USA) Columbia CK 90732

Chet Baker – tp
Jean-Jacques Goldman – voc
G. Delacroix – b
J.Y. D'Angelo – p
R. Romanelli – synth, acc
C. Deschamps – dr

Paris (F), July 1985
5 Parler d'ma vie

Round Midnight (Soundtrack)
CBS CD 70300
(USA) Columbia CK 40464
(J) Sony/CBS 32DP-547

Chet Baker – tp, voc
Herbie Hancock – p
Pierre Michelot – b
Billy Higgins – dr

Epinay sur Seine (F), July 1985
4 Fair weather

Rique Pantoja E Chet Baker
(BR) WEA 255155-2
(USA) Tropical Storm/
WEA Latina WH 55155
(J) Canyon D22Y-0342

Chet Baker – tp, voc on 4
Rique Pantoja – keyb, synth, p, voc on 4
Sizao Machado – b
Bob Wyatt – dr
Silvano Michelino – perc on 1, 2

Rio de Janeiro/São Paulo (BR), 1985/1987
1 *Cinema 1*
2 *Saci [Brazilian Goblin]*
4 *So hard to know*
5 *Te Cantei [I made a pass at you]*

Lizzy Mercier Descloux
One For The Soul
(F) Polydor 827 910-2
(J) Polydor P33P-20062
(J) Polydor POCP-2220

Chet Baker – tp
Lizzy Mercier Descloux – voc
Leonardo Gandelman – sax
Moacyr Marques da Silva – bcl
Sivuca – acc
Luiz Fernando M. Lima – p
Vincent Bouvot – keyb
Doudeth "Neco" de Azevedo – g
Vitor Biglione, Zeppa – eg
Jamil Jones, Dos Santos, Jorge Degas,
Harry Bruce – b
Billy Perry, Paulo Braga – dr
Alceu Maia – cavaquinho, perc, backvoc
Djalma Correa, Marcelo Salazar,
Paulo "Chacal" Perira – perc
Michel Cron – vl
Jose Luiz Maziotti, Adam Kidron,
Slim Batteux, Lorenza Johnson – backvoc

Rio de Janeiro (BR), July/August 1985
3 *Fog horn Blues*
5 *My funny Valentine*
7 *Garden of Alas*
9 *Off off pleasure*
11 *Love streams*

Seven Faces Of Valentine
(I) Philology W 30-2

Chet Baker – tp, voc
Edy Olivieri – p
Ilario de Marinis – b
Vincenzo Mazzone – dr

Locorotondo (I), Sept 1985
7 My funny Valentine

Ghiglione/Melillo/Baker
Goodbye, Chet
(I) Philology W 22-2

Chet Baker – tp
Tiziana Ghiglione – voc
Edy Olivieri – p
Ilario de Marinis – b
Vincenzo Mazzone – dr

Bari (I), Sept 6, 1985
12 Lament

Bari (I), Sept 7, 1985
13 Lament

Naima (The Unusual Chet/Vol. 1)
(I) Philology W 52-2

Chet Baker – tp
and Jazz Studio Orchestra:
Martino Chiarulli, Guiseppe Caldarcia,
Mario Trizio, Mino Laciriguela – tp
Mario Concetto Andriulli – tp on 3, 5
Nucci Guerra, Muzio Petrella,
Giovanni Pellegrini,
Gaetano Bisceglie – tb
Guiseppe Congedo, Pino Pichierri,
Nicola Nitti, Silvano Martina,
Michele Consueto – sax
Sal Nistico – ts on 3
Edy Olivieri – p
Ilario de Marinis – b
Vincenzo Mazzone – dr
Lino Musso – perc
Paolo Lepore – cond

Bari (I), Sept 7, 1985
3 Killer Joe
5 A child is born

Bari (I), Sept 10, 1985
4 Lover man

Chet Baker in Europe
(D) b&w bwcd 001

Chet Baker – tp
Edu Ninck Blok – co, tp
Evert Hekkema – bh
Kees van Lier – as
Dick de Graaf – ts
Jan Vennik – bs
Bert van den Brink – p
Hein Van de Geyn – b
John Engels – dr

Loenen a/d Vecht (NL), Sept 22, 1985
5 Someday you'll leave me
6 Deep soul
7 Shifting down
8 Tergiversation

Chet Baker Sings Again
(NL) Timeless CDSJP 238
(J) Baystate R32J-1019
(J) Baystate BVCJ-5016

Chet Baker – tp, voc
Michel Graillier – p
Riccardo Del Fra – b
John Engels – dr

Monster (NL), Oct 2/8, 1985
1 All of you
2 Body and soul
3 Look for the silver lining
4 I can't get started
5 My funny Valentine
6 Alone together
7 Someone to watch over me
8 How deep is the ocean

Heartbreak
(NL) Timeless CDSJP 366
(J) Alfa Timeless ALCR-109

Chet Baker – tp, voc
Michel Graillier – p
Riccardo Del Fra – b
John Engels – dr
+ strings (overdubbed)

Monster (NL), Oct 2/8, 1985
(overdubbed in 1991)
2 All of you
3 My funny Valentine

Mister B
(NL) Timeless CDSJP 192
Re-release contains the six tracks
recorded on May 25, 1983 plus

Chet Baker – tp
Michel Graillier – p
Riccardo Del Fra – b

Monster (NL), Oct 4, 1985
7 White Blues

Chet Baker – tp
Michel Graillier – p
Riccardo Del Fra – b
Philip Catherine – g

Monster (NL), Dec 12, 1985
8 Father X-mas

Live From The Moonlight
(I) Philology W 10/11-2

Chet Baker – tp, voc on 4 (Disc 1)
on 3, 4 (Disc 2)
Michel Graillier – p
Massimo Moriconi – b

Macerata (I), Nov 24, 1985
Disc 1
1 Polka dots and moonbeams
2 Night bird
3 Estate
4 Polka dots and moonbeams
5 Arborway

Disc 2
1 Dee's dilemma
2 How deep is the ocean
3 My foolish heart
4 My funny Valentine
5 Broken wing
6 Funk in deep freeze

Lou Donaldson, Sal Nistico,
CB, Woody Shaw, Dizzy Gillespie
Verona (I) · Jan 1985
Elena Carminati

Woody Shaw + CB
Verona (I) · Jan 1985
88   *Elena Carminati*

CB, Kristán Magnússon,
Tómas R. Einarsson

Kristján Magnússon, CB,
Tómas R. Einarsson, Sveinn Óli Jónsson
Reykjavík (IS)/Gamla Bio · Feb 2, 1985
Ingimundur Magnússon

Toots Thielemans, CB,
Kjell Jansson, Åke Johansson
Västerås (S) · Feb 1985
90   *Gunnar Holmberg*

København (DK)/Montmartre
Feb 28, 1985
Gorm Valentin

Jesper Lundgaard

*The first time I met Chet Baker in 1982
was at the "Montmartre" in Copenhagen.
That evening, Doug Raney, Horace Parlan,
Alex Riel and I formed a quartet that was
supposed to accompany Chet.*

*I had been told that Chet could be very
difficult to work with but, that evening,
everything fell into place from the very
first note that we played, and I enjoyed it
immensely.*

*Later, I had some not so nice experi-
ences with Chet, partly caused by his self-
destructive habits, sometimes resulting in
him not showing up at concerts, sometimes
resulting in performances that did not
come up to his normal artistic level.*

*Anyway, he always managed to get a
lot of atmosphere and feeling into his
music, no matter the circumstances, and
for me it was a great learning experience.*

*Looking back, it is easier to remember
the good than the bad times, and I am
proud to have been one of his sidemen.*

Das erste Mal begegnete ich Chet Baker 1982 im „Montmartre" in
Kopenhagen. Ich spielte zusammen mit Doug Raney, Horace Parlan und
Alex Riel in einem Quartett, das Chet begleiten sollte.

Man hatte mir gesagt, daß es mitunter schwierig sei, mit Chet zu
arbeiten, aber an jenem Abend klappte alles reibungslos, von der ersten
Note an, und ich genoß es sehr.

Später machte ich dann einige weniger schöne Erfahrungen mit Chet,
die zum Teil auf seiner selbstzerstörerischen Lebensweise beruhten:
Mitunter tauchte er zu Konzerten einfach nicht auf, in anderen Fällen
blieb er unterhalb seines üblichen künstlerischen Niveaus.

Trotzdem gelang es ihm immer, seiner Musik Atmosphäre und Gefühl
zu geben, egal, unter welchen Bedingungen, und ich habe damals viel
gelernt.

Wenn man zurückblickt, erinnert man sich lieber an die guten als an
die schlechten Zeiten, und ich bin stolz, mit ihm gespielt zu haben.

Doug Raney, Jesper Lundgaard, CB
København (DK)/Montmartre
Feb 28, 1985
Gorm Valentin   *Übersetzung: Caroline Mähl*

Amsterdam (NL)/De Kroeg
March 3, 1985
Gert de Ruyter

Philip Catherine,
Jean-Louis Rassinfosse, CB
San Remo (I) · April 1985
94 *Elena Carminati*

Ivrea (I) · April 1985
Elena Carminati

Stockholm (S) / Skeppsholmen
June 29, 1985
Gunnar Holmberg

Orchestra Filarmonica Marchigiani,
CB + Jacques Pelzer
Macerata (I) · July 2, 1985
Carlo Pieroni

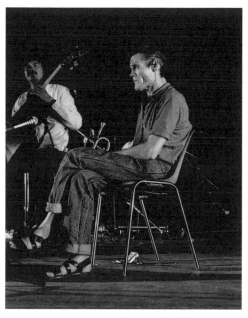

Jean-Louis Rassinfosse *

Für mich ist die Erinnerung an Chet geprägt von seiner strikten Musikalität: Für ihn war alles Musik, er schien immer hellwach zu sein. Im Auto sangen wir zusammen, die ganze Zeit . . . Und natürlich von der Ernsthaftigkeit seiner Musik: Jede Note hat Gewicht, es gibt keinen Platz für Geplapper in seiner Sprache, es zählt nur das Wesentliche, und auch das ist genau durchdacht. Er war einer von denen, die sehr viel über Musik reflektierten, obwohl ihn die Öffentlichkeit meist anders einstufte: „Na gut, er spielte nach dem Gehör, er war ein großartiger Improvisator." Er machte sich Gedanken über die Wahl der Noten und wie man Räume mit ihnen füllt.

Natürlich habe ich auch viele persönliche Erinnerungen an ihn, schließlich haben wir mehr als zehn Jahre zusammengearbeitet. Für mich war er wirklich, im wörtlichen Sinne, ein außergewöhnlicher Mensch, er bewegte sich abseits der ausgetretenen Pfade, hatte mit überholten Normen nichts zu tun. Und er besaß eine Großzügigkeit, eine Menschlichkeit, die unabhängig von seiner Person existierten, die das Leben so sehr gebeutelt hatte. Er hat sich trotzdem immer eine Art Naivität bewahrt. Mir kam er manchmal vor wie ein Ritter aus dem Mittelalter, mit seinem ungeheuren Gerechtigkeitssinn und Ehrempfinden und seinem Erstaunen darüber, daß es tatsächlich Menschen gab, die ihm übelgesinnt waren.

What I remember most clearly about Chet is his rigorous musicality; for him everything was music, his mind seemed to be working constantly. In the car we used to sing together, all the time . . . And, of course, the seriousness of his music: every note is weighted, chattiness has no place in his language, everything is reduced to the essential, and that, too, has been considered carefully. He reflected a lot about music although people used to have a different picture of him: "Oh well, he plays by ear, he's a great improvisor." He was thinking about the choice of notes and how they should be arranged in space.

Naturally, I also have a lot of memories on the personal level, after all we worked together for more than ten years. For me he was, quite literally, an outstanding person; he avoided the beaten track, he didn't care about outmoded rules. And he had a generosity, a humanity about him which existed independently from the person that life had treated so badly. He had, in spite of all that, retained a kind of naivety. Sometimes he appeared to me like a medieval knight, with his incredible sense of justice and honour, his amazement at the fact that there were people who were ripping him off.

Philip Catherine,
Jean-Louis Rassinfosse, CB
Messina (I) · Sept. 4, 1985
Nino Leotta

Übersetzung: Klemens Berthold
*aus „Jazz in Time", Juli / August 1989

Translation: Caroline Mähl
*from "Jazz in Time", July / August 1989

Evert Hekkema

Chet was playing a concert in a small club in Amsterdam. There were about 200 people present in a cramped space. By the time I arrived there was an intermission and I found Chet at the entrance door, sweating. He gave me a rueful smile that seemed to allude to the hubbub emanating from the club. We talked for a while and then went in for the next set.

Chet said: "Follow me to the stage, it's the safest place in the joint." The crowd opened up, and there I sat – on Chet's trumpet case. Chet sat down on a chair, as usual. He played a tune, sang another, scatted some, took it out, and then, to my surprise, introduced me to the audience and handed his horn over to me. The mouthpiece was smaller than my own but what else could I do but play? For two tunes I was Chet Baker. It almost made me sing.

Chet spielte in einem kleinen Club in Amsterdam, in dem sich ungefähr zweihundert Leute drängelten. Als ich eintraf, war gerade Pause, und Chet stand schwitzend am Eingang. Er schenkte mir ein trübseliges Lächeln, das sich wohl auf den Tumult bezog, der von drinnen zu hören war. Wir unterhielten uns eine Weile und gingen wieder hinein, als der nächste Set anstand.

Chet sagte: „Komm mit mir auf die Bühne, das ist der sicherste Ort in diesem Laden." Die Menge machte uns Platz, und ich fand mich auf Chets Trompetenkoffer wieder. Chet setzte sich wie üblich auf einen Stuhl. Er spielte ein Stück, sang ein weiteres, scattete ein bißchen, kam in Fahrt, und dann, zu meiner Verblüffung, stellte er mich dem Publikum vor und überreichte mir sein Horn. Das Mundstück war kleiner als meines, aber was konnte ich schon anderes tun als spielen? Zwei Stücke lang war ich Chet Baker. Fast hätte ich zu singen angefangen.

Übersetzung: Caroline Mähl

Die erste Begegnung zwischen Chet und dem Amstel Octet fand im August 1984 statt, als die Band für ihr erstes Album probte. Die meisten von uns hatten bereits bei Konzerten oder Aufnahmen mit Chet gearbeitet. Evert war im Laufe der Jahre zu einem guten Freund Chets geworden und hatte ihn 1983 auf einer Italien-Tournee begleitet. Er spielte Chet unsere Platte zu Hause vor, und da sie ihm gefiel, luden wir ihn über Evert ein, auf unserem nächsten Album als Solist mitzuspielen. Er willigte ein, und der Termin für die Aufnahme wurde auf den 22. September gelegt. In den Tagen davor fragte ich mich manchmal: „Wird er kommen?". An jenem Sonntagmorgen hörte ich von Evert, daß Chet ihn gerade von Liège aus angerufen habe, wo er bei den Pelzers wohnte, und daß er ins Studio komme. Um zwei Uhr nachmittags traf er ein, in einem Alfa Romeo.

Edu Ninck Blok*

Chet and the Amstel Octet first met in August 1984 when the band was rehearsing for its first record. Most of us had worked with Chet on different occasions varying from live concerts to recordings. Evert had become a personal friend of Chet over the years, and in 1983 he joined Chet on a tour in Italy. Chet heard our record at Evert's home and he liked it. Through Evert we invited him to be the featured soloist on our next album, and Chet agreed. The date was set for September 22, and for a couple of days I found myself asking, Will he come? That Sunday morning Evert told me that Chet had just phoned him from Liège where he stayed with the Pelzer family and that he would come to the studio. At two p.m. he arrived in an Alfa Romeo.

Jan Vennik, Evert Hekkema, CB,
Bert van den Brink, Hein Van de Geyn,
Kees van Lier, John Engels,
Edu Ninck Blok, Dick de Graaf
Loenen a/d Vecht (NL) · Sept 22, 1985
Archive E.N.B.

Übersetzung: Caroline Mähl
*aus den Liner Notes zu „Hazy Hugs"
mit dem Amstel Octet

*from the liner notes for "Hazy Hugs"
by the Amstel Octet

Philip Catherine + CB
Zagreb (YUG) · Oct 25, 1985

100 *Mladen Mazur*

Riccardo Del Fra + CB
Hamburg (D)/Fabrik · Nov 10, 1985
Harald Koch

Rolf Ericson, Maffy Falay, CB
Stockholm (S) / Fasching · Nov 1985
Gunnar Holmberg

Michel Graillier + CB
Macerata (I) · Nov 24, 1985
102 *Carlo Pieroni*

Michel Graillier*

Man hat Chet oft vorgeworfen, seine Musik sei altmodisch, aber ich glaube eher, daß es die Leute waren, die ein bißchen überholt dachten. Chet konnte erst anfangen zu spielen, wenn er eine gewisse Aufgeschlossenheit für seine Musik spürte, eine bestimmte Form der Aufmerksamkeit. In Japan, wo das Publikum viel disziplinierter ist als bei uns, dauerte das selten länger als fünf Minuten, aber in Frankreich oder in den USA wartete er manchmal länger als eine halbe Stunde, bis der Lärm im Saal abnahm und die äußerliche Spannung sich legte. Bei Clubauftritten zum Beispiel kam es häufig vor, daß die Leute unruhig waren und dem, was sich auf der Bühne abspielte, wenig Interesse entgegenbrachten. So etwas konnte Chet nicht ertragen. Er sagte immer: „Je lauter die Leute sind, desto leiser muß man spielen." Wenn ihm das Publikum zu unkonzentriert war, machte er eine Pause, bis der Lärm aufhörte. Von seinen Musikern verlangte er etwas Ähnliches, eine Art tonaler Askese. Für einen Pianisten ist es einfach zu brillieren – der Umfang des Instruments ist groß, und mit guter Technik kann man schneller spielen als auf den meisten anderen Instrumenten. Mitunter neigte ich ein wenig dazu, mich von meinem pianistischen Ehrgeiz hinreißen zu lassen. Ich kann mich erinnern, daß ich während eines Konzerts einmal eine ziemlich virtuose Einlage brachte. Chet ergriff daraufhin das Mikrofon und sagte mir auf offener Bühne: „Mensch, Michel, was willst du uns beweisen?" So eine Lektion vergißt man nicht!

People have often accused Chet of playing old-fashioned music but I'm inclined to believe that it was rather such listeners whose thinking was outmoded. Chet could only start playing when he felt that an atmosphere of receptiveness had been established, a certain quality of attention. In Japan, where the audience is much more disciplined, this process rarely took longer than five minutes but in France or in the USA he waited sometimes for more than half an hour until the noise died down and external tensions diminished. At club gigs, for example, it happened quite often that people were chatting and not much interested in what went on on the stage. Chet could not endure this. He used to tell me: "The louder people get the quieter you have to play." If he thought the audience was not attentive enough he paused and waited for the racket to stop. Of his musicians he expected something similar, a kind of tonal asceticism. It is easy for a pianist to shine – the instrument has a large range, and with a good technique you can play faster than on most other instruments. Sometimes I could be overwhelmed by my pianistic fervour. I remember that once, during a concert, I played a rather virtuosic interlude. Chet took the microphone and said, in front of the audience: "Hey, Michel, what do you want to prove by that?" That's the kind of lesson you'll never forget!

Übersetzung: Klemens Berthold
*aus „Jazz Magazine", Juli/August 1990

Translation: Caroline Mähl
*from "Jazz Magazine", July/August 1990

London (GB) / Ronnie Scott's
Nov 25, 1985
104   *Allan Titmuss*

Kiel (D)/Pumpe · Dec 6, 1985
Thilo Corts

Christopher Mason/Chet Baker
Silent Nights – A Christmas Album
(CDN) Varrick CD-032
(J) A32C-88
(J) Teichiku TECX-25020

Chet Baker – tp
Christopher Mason – as
Mike Pellera – p
Jim Singleton – b
Johnny Vidacovitch – dr

New Orleans, La. (USA), Jan 7, 1986
1 Silent night pt.1
2 The first noel
3 We three kings
4 Hark, the herald angels sing
5 Nobody knows the trouble I've seen
6 Amazing grace
7 Come all ye faithful
8 Joy to the world
9 Amen
10 It came upon a midnight clear
11 Swing low sweet chariot
12 Silent night pt.2

When Sunny Gets Blue
(DK) SteepleChase SCCD-31221
(J) SteepleChase VACE-1062

Chet Baker – tp, voc on 7
Butch Lacy – p
Jesper Lundgaard – b
Jukkis Uotila – dr

København (DK), Feb 23, 1986
1 Long ago and far away
2 Here's that rainy day
3 Two in the dew
4 I should care
5 Out of nowhere
6 When sunny gets blue
7 Isn't it romantic
8 You'd be so nice to come home

Live At Ronnie Scott's
(GB) Wadham WHCD 003
(GB) Hendring HEN 6044 Y
(J) Jazz Road BY32-5010
Night Bird
(GB) Castle Communication ESMCD 015

Chet Baker – tp, voc on 1,4
Michel Graillier – p
Riccardo Del Fra – b
Van Morrison – voc on 9

London (GB), June 6, 1986
1 But not for me
2 Arborway
3 If I should lose you
4 My ideal
5 Night bird
6 Love for sale
7 Shifting down
8 You can't go home again
9 Send in the clowns

Singin' In The Midnight
(J) Polydor KK J33J-20153

Chet Baker – tp, voc on 1,2,4,6,8
Harold Danko – p
Jon Burr – b
Ben Riley – dr

Monster (NL), Dec 17-19, 1986
1 Blue moon
2 My foolish heart
3 When she smiles
4 My melancholy baby
5 Sea breeze
6 For all we know
7 Swift shifting
8 Round midnight

Love Song
(J) RVC/Baystate R32J-1065
(J) Baystate BVCJ-5021

Chet Baker – tp, voc on 1,2,4-6
Harold Danko – p
Jon Burr – b
Ben Riley – dr

Monster (NL), Dec 17-19, 1986
1 I'm a fool to want you
2 You and the night and the music
3 Round midnight
4 As time goes by
5 You'd be so nice to come home to
6 Angel eyes
7 Caravelle

Cool Cat
(NL) Timeless CDSJP 262
As Time Goes By
(NL) Timeless CDSJP 251/252

Chet Baker – tp
Harold Danko – p
Jon Burr – b
Ben Riley – dr

Monster (NL), Dec 17-19, 1986
7 You have been here all along

"Singin' In The Midnight" and "Love Song" were originally released in Japan. The same material appeared later in two different compilations, "Cool Cat" and "As Time Goes By", for the European market. The latter features one track not contained on the Japanese editions.

Heartbreak
(NL) Timeless CDSJP 366
(J) Alfa Timeless ALCR-109

Chet Baker – tp, voc
Harold Danko – p
Jon Burr – b
Ben Riley – dr
+ strings (overdubbed)

Monster (NL), Dec 17-19, 1986
(overdubbed in 1991)
1 Angel eyes
4 Blue moon
5 I'm a fool to want you
6 You and the night and the music
7 As time goes by
8 Round midnight
9 My melancholy baby
10 My foolish heart

Listening to the band of Pierre Voiana (sax)
Liège (B)/Lion s'Envoile · Feb 24, 1986
Philippe Gielen

(Urgent)

Write a letter to Jackie about getting another copy of all his pictures of myself and Diane. Diane and I, as large as possible.

◀ Diane Vavra + CB
Liège (B) · March 1986
110 *Jacky Lepage*

CB, Diane Vavra, Jacques Pelzer
Liège (B) · March 1986
Jacky Lepage

Jacques Pelzer + CB
Liège (B) · March 1986
Jacky Lepage

III

Liège (B) · March 1986
112   *Jacky Lepage*

Liège (B) · March 1986
Jacky Lepage

Paris (F) / New Morning · April 9, 1986
Michel Becret

Daß ich heute in Frankreich lebe, daß ich international „Karriere" gemacht habe, ist zum großen Teil Chets Verdienst. Die Musik, die ich heute schreibe oder spiele – ob Jazz-Standards oder neue Kompositionen –, ist von den Begegnungen mit Chet geprägt. Mein Verhältnis zu ihm läßt sich, glaube ich, mit dem vergleichen, was Dave Liebman über seine Erfahrungen mit Miles gesagt hat: In seiner Gruppe zu spielen und mit ihm auf Tour zu gehen, war ein echter Gewaltakt, der physische, psychische und moralische Stärke erforderte. Aber dafür wurde ich mehr als entschädigt.

Chet war ein Mensch von ungewöhnlicher Eleganz, anspruchsvoll, intelligent und großzügig. Ein Künstler im wahrsten Sinne des Wortes, ein mutiger Mensch und „jünger" als all seine Altersgenossen.

Riccardo Del Fra*

That I live in France, that my "career" is international, is to a large extent thanks to Chet. The music that I write and play today, whether jazz standards or new compositions, is influenced by the encounters with Chet. My relationship to him is comparable, in a way, to what Dave Liebman said of his work with Miles: to play in his group and go on tour with him was a real tour-de-force that required physical, psychological and moral strength. The benefits, however, more than compensated for the necessary commitment.

Chet was a man of unusual elegance, demanding, intelligent, and generous. An artist in the true meaning of the word, courageous, and "younger" than all his contemporaries.

Riccardo Del Fra + CB
Bruxelles (B)/Bothanique · April 11, 1986
Jacky Lepage

Übersetzung: Giuseppe de Siati
*aus „Chet Baker in Italia"

Translation: Caroline Mahl
*from "Chet Baker in Italia"

Hamburg (D)/Fabrik · April 15, 1986

Michael Steen

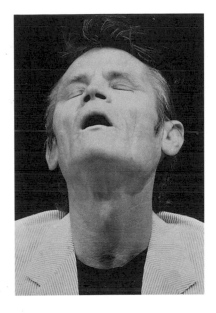

Pori (SF) · July 12, 1986
Timo Pylvänäinen (Lehtikuva Oy)

London (GB)/Ronnie Scott's
August 11, 1986
Allan Titmuss

London (GB) / Ronnie Scott's
August 21, 1986
Allan Titmuss

Paul Witte, CB, Leo Mitchell
Rotterdam (NL) / Thelonious
Aug 30, 1986
Hajo Piebenga   **119**

Let's Get Lost (Soundtrack)
RCA PD-83054
(USA) RCA/Novus 3054-2-N
(J) RCA R32J-1088

Chet Baker – tp, voc
Frank Strazzeri – p
John Leftwich – b
Ralph Penland – dr, perc on 1, 4-6

Hollywood, Cal. (USA), Jan 1987
1 Moon and sand
2 Imagination
4 For heaven's sake
5 Everytime we say goodbye
6 I don't stand a ghost of a chance with you
7 Daydream
9 Blame it on my youth
10 My one and only love

Chet Baker – tp on 8, voc on 3, 11, 12
Frank Strazzeri – p
John Leftwich – b
Ralph Penland – dr, perc on 3
Nicola Stilo – fl, g on 8

Paris (F), May 1987
3 You're my thrill
8 Zingaro
[a/k/a Portrait in black and white]
11 Everything happens to me
12 Almost blue

A Night At The Shalimar
(I) Philology W 59-2

Chet Baker – tp, voc on 3
Mike Melillo – p on 1-3
Luca Flores – p on 4-6
Nicola Stilo – fl
Furio di Castri – b

Senigallia (I), May 23, 1987
1 Mr. B
2 Arbor way
3 Just friends
4 Night bird
5 Conception
6 I remember you

Seven Faces Of Valentine
(I) Philology W 30-2

Chet Baker – tp, voc
Nicola Stilo – fl
Mike Melillo – p
Furio di Castri – b

Senigallia (I), May 23, 1987
5 My funny Valentine

Chet Baker In Tokyo – Memories
(J) King K32Y-6270

Chet Baker – tp, voc on 3, 5
Harold Danko – p
Hein Van de Geyn – b
John Engels – dr

Tokyo (J), June 14, 1987
1 Stella by starlight
2 For minors only
3 Almost blue
4 Portrait in black and white
5 My funny Valentine

Chet Baker In Tokyo – Four
(J) King K32Y-6281

Chet Baker – tp, voc on 3, 5
Harold Danko – p
Hein Van de Geyn – b
John Engels – dr

Tokyo (J), June 14, 1987
1 Four
2 Arbor way
3 I'm a fool to want you
4 Seven steps to heaven
5 For all we know
6 Broken wing

Naima (The Unusual Chet/Vol. I)
(I) Philology W 52-2

Chet Baker – tp
Tom Harrell – tp
Hal Galper – p
Steve Gilmore – b
Bill Goodwin – dr

Modena (I), July 20, 1987
2 Mr. B

Chet Baker – tp
Kirk Lightsey – p
Rocky Knauer – b

Tarcento (I), Aug 1987
7 Naima

Chet Baker & Wolfgang Lackerschmid Originals
(D) art & sound as-j 001
Welcome Back
(D) West Wind CD 2083

Chet Baker – tp
Wolfgang Lackerschmid – vib, arr
Günter Lenz – b on 1, 2, 4, 6-8
Nicola Stilo – fl, g on 2, 5, 6, 8
Peri dos Santos – g on 3, 5
Rocky Knauer – b on 3, 5
Edir dos Santos – dr on 3, 5

Bischofsmais (D), Aug 24-26, 1987
1 Welcome back
2 Christmas Waltz
3 Glorias answer
4 Pitztal daybreak
5 Volta trais
6 Try it dry
7 Why shouldn't you cry
8 Waltz for Berlin

Charlie Haden
Silence
(I) Soul Note 121 172-2

Chet Baker – tp, voc on 4
Enrico Pieranunzi – p
Charlie Haden – b
Billy Higgins – dr

Roma (I), Dec 11 / 12, 1987
1 Visa
2 Silence
3 Echi
4 My funny Valentine
5 Round about midnight
6 Conception

Naima (The Unusual Chet / Vol. 1)
(I) Philology W 52-2

Chet Baker – tp
Enrico Pieranunzi – p
Massimo Moriconi – b
John Arnold – dr

Ostia (I), Nov 1987
6 Seven steps to heaven

Straight From The Heart
(D) Enja 6020-2
(USA) Rhino R21S-79624
(J) Enja ENJ-22

Chet Baker – tp, voc
Walter Norris – p
Lucas Lindholm – b

Hamburg (D), Nov 14, 1987
7 My funny Valentine

Felice Reggio
I Remember Chet
(I) Philology W 111.2

Chet Baker – tp, p
Nicola Stilo – g
Rocky Knauer – b

Pordenone (I), Nov 30, 1987
9 Portrait in black and white

Paris (F) / Passage de l'Industrie
Feb 14, 1987
Philippe Cibille

Jon Burr

*Chet und ich trugen damals beide an der Last der Sucht. Wir glaubten,
daß die Zustände, in denen man die beste Musik macht, nur durch
Drogen hervorgerufen werden könnten und daß wir mit dem Konsum von
Drogen irgendwie einer großen Sache dienten – „der Musik" zum
Beispiel – und uns freiwillig auf dem Altar der Kunst opferten.*

*Heute repräsentieren wir zwei von drei möglichen Ergebnissen der
Sucht. Chet ist tot, ich bin clean. Die dritte Möglichkeit ist Einlieferung –
in ein Gefängnis, ein Krankenhaus oder ähnliches. Ich danke Gott für
meine drogenfreie Existenz.*

*Mir ist klar geworden, daß die Fähigkeit des Zuhörens das wichtigste
beim Spielen ist und daß es dabei ebenso viele Abstufungen wie Musiker
gibt. Es ist etwas, das gelernt und geübt werden kann, eine mentale
Technik, wenn man so will, aber auch ein Geschenk.*

*Chet besaß diese Fähigkeit in hohem Maße – höher als bei fast allen
Musikern, die ich kenne oder spielen gehört habe. Er horchte ganz tief in
seinen Klang hinein und gab ihm die Transparenz, die nur bei absoluter
Tonreinheit möglich ist. Er behauptete, er hätte keinen blassen Schim-
mer, was ein C^7-Akkord ist, aber er konnte ihn hören, und er hörte mehr
darin als die meisten anderen. Das Tragische an Chets Tod ist, daß er auf
der Suche nach etwas gestorben ist, das er längst besaß.*

*In those days Chet and I shared the burden
of addiction. We had this belief that the
states of being which produced the best
music were induced by drugs, and thought
that by using drugs we were somehow
serving some larger cause, like "the Music",
sacrificing ourselves willingly for "Art".*

*Today we manifest two of the three
possible outcomes of addiction. Chet is
dead; I am sober. The third outcome is
institutionalization, as in jails, hospitals,
etc. I thank God for my sobriety.*

*I've come to realize that the degree of
listening is paramount in musical perform-
ance, and that there are as many degrees
as there are performers. It is a mental
skill; a discipline that can be developed
and practised; a psychic technique, if you
will, as well as a gift.*

*Chet had this skill to a high degree –
higher than almost all musicians I've
known or heard. He heard all the way into
his sound, giving it the translucence which
comes from perfection of pitch. He
claimed not to know a C from a hole in
the ground but he heard it, and heard more
in it than most. The cruel tragedy of Chet's
death is that he died in search of something he already possessed.*

Übersetzung: Caroline Mähl

Jon Burr + CB
Köln (D) / Subway · Feb 16, 1987
Hyou Vielz

Maurice Cullaz + CB
Billancourt (F)
Théâtre de Boulogne Billancourt
May 1987
124   *Philippe Cibille*

Tom Harrell, CB, Steve Gilmore
Modena (I) · July 20, 1987
Carlo Pieroni

Hilversum (NL)/Theater Gooiland
Sept 5, 1987

Gert de Ruyter

Amsterdam (NL) · Sept 22, 1987
Gert de Ruyter

Diane Vavra + CB
Istanbul (TR) / Airport · Sept 26, 1987
128   *Cumhuriyet archive*

Dortmund (D)/Domicil · Oct 5, 1987
Uwe Killing

Antwerpen (B)/Riverside · Oct 18, 1987

Jacky Lepage

Im nachhinein hat man viel über die Zerbrechlichkeit Chet Bakers
geredet. Pure Erfindung! Im Gegenteil, er war eine Naturgewalt.
Ich habe ihn mit nacktem Oberkörper gesehen – er hatte die Muskulatur
eines Athleten. Auch sein Trompetenspiel hatte nichts Schwächliches an
sich. Ich weiß nicht, woher die Kritiker dieses Bild von dünnem Ton und
abnehmender Klangfülle nehmen. Es reicht, wenn man sich die Aufnahmen anhört: Der Klang ist immer voll, klar und mächtig. Der Eindruck
von Schwäche entstand dadurch, daß er jegliche Art von Effekt ablehnte;
alles Spektakuläre, das durch starke Schwankungen in der Dynamik entsteht, empfand er als zu einfach und eines guten Trompeters unwürdig.
Wenn man bedenkt, wie viele Platten Chet bis an sein Lebensende
eingespielt und wie viele Konzerte er gegeben hat, wird einem klar,
wieviel physische Widerstandskraft er besaß. Er konnte ungeheure Kräfte
mobilisieren, weil sein Bedürfnis zu spielen unstillbar war.

Er war ein Hitzkopf, stammte aus Oklahoma und fühlte sich immer
noch als Cowboy . . . Auf jeden Fall war er alles andere als ein Verlierer
oder ein gebrochener Mann. Aber wenn es um Jazz geht, ziehen die
Leute morbide Geschichten eben vor.

Michel Graillier*

*After his death there was a lot of talk
about Chet Baker's fragility. Pure fantasy!
On the contrary, he was a force of nature.
I once saw him stripped to the waist – he
had the muscles of an athlete. His trumpet
playing, too, had nothing feeble about it.
I don't know where the critics got this
image of a thin tone and weakening sound
from. It's enough to listen to the recordings: the sound is always strong, pure and
powerful. The impression of feebleness
resulted from his never straining for effect.
Anything showy based on strong dynamic
variations he rejected as being too simple
a solution for a good trumpeter. If you
think of the many albums Chet recorded
right until the end of his life, the many
concerts he played, you realize how much
stamina he had. He could mobilize
incredible physical strength because his
desire to play was insatiable.*

*He was a hotspur, he came from
Oklahoma and still saw himself as a cowboy . . . At any rate, he was anything but a
loser or a defeated man. But when it
comes to jazz, people prefer the morbid
stories.*

Übersetzung: Klemens Berthold
*aus „Jazz Magazine", Juli/August 1990

Michel Graillier
Antwerpen (B)/Riverside · Oct 18, 1987
Jacky Lepage

Translation: Caroline Mähl
*from "Jazz Magazine", July/August 1990

Rocky Knauer

As long as I knew him he was living from suitcases until, shortly before his tragic death, Chet and Diane found an apartment in Paris and he finally bought a car. He loved to drive and had always wanted his own car. One time in Paris, Chet proved to me what an excellent driver he was, in any condition. He had just received his medicine from a doctor in Montparnasse and was feeling good. We had ten minutes to get to the club "Le Dreher" in Châtelet. There was a huge traffic jam all the way down Blvd St-Michel to the river. Chet would see a space about ten cars ahead, pull out into the wrong side of the street, drive full speed and then make a screeching halt into the space. Then he'd drive to the right, onto the sidewalk, through the traffic light and back into the street. This procedure continued at high speed until we got to the club. I couldn't believe it! He had full control all the time and didn't endanger anyone. We were there in five minutes!

As far as I remember there was never a dull moment – except for some of the long waits for a train or an airplane. It was always a pleasure being on the road with Chet. The hotels were usually very good, the promoters treated us with respect and would invite the band to a good supper. Chet also took good care of the band, making sure we had everything we needed, and I can remember many a day when he treated us to an excellent meal. I had the opportunity, or maybe it was just good fortune, to travel with Chet through practically every country in Europe, from the south of Sicily to the polar regions of Sweden, meeting a lot of nice people and great musicians. The last concert with Chet, and the last time I saw him, was at the Hannover Jazz Club on January 4, 1988. To me Chet Baker was a sweet and soft-spoken, straightforward and warm-hearted man. I could talk about the dark side, the drug side, but enough people have done that.

Solange ich Chet kannte, lebte er aus dem Koffer. Erst kurz vor seinem tragischen Tod fanden er und Diane eine Wohnung in Paris, und Chet kaufte sich endlich ein Auto. Er fuhr gern und hatte sich immer einen eigenen Wagen gewünscht. Einmal bewies er mir in Paris, was für ein guter Fahrer er war, in jedem Zustand. Er hatte von einem Doktor in Montparnasse gerade seine Medizin bekommen und fühlte sich gut. Wir hatten zehn Minuten Zeit, um in den Club „Le Dreher" in Châtelet zu kommen, und der Boulevard St-Michel war bis hinunter zur Seine völlig verstopft. Sobald Chet eine Lücke sah, zehn Autos weiter vorn, wechselte er auf die Gegenfahrbahn, fuhr fünfzig Meter mit Vollgas und kam mit quietschenden Reifen in der Lücke zum Stehen. Dann wechselte er nach rechts, auf den Bürgersteig, fuhr über die rote Ampel und zurück auf die Straße. So ging es mit höchster Geschwindigkeit bis zum Club weiter. Ich konnte es nicht fassen! Er hatte die ganze Zeit über alles unter Kontrolle und gefährdete niemanden. Wir hatten nur fünf Minuten gebraucht!

Soweit ich mich erinnere, wurde es nie langweilig – mit Ausnahme langer Wartezeiten auf Bahnhöfen oder Flughäfen. Die Hotels waren meist sehr gut, die Veranstalter behandelten uns mit Respekt und servierten abends etwas Anständiges zu essen. Chet kümmerte sich um die Band, sorgte dafür, daß wir alles bekamen, was wir brauchten, und lud uns öfter zu einem exzellenten Mahl ein. Ich hatte die Gelegenheit – vielleicht war es auch einfach nur Glück –, mit Chet durch praktisch alle Länder Europas zu reisen, von der Südküste Siziliens bis zum äußersten Norden Schwedens, und ich habe dabei eine Menge netter Leute und großartiger Musiker kennengelernt. Das letzte Konzert mit Chet fand am 4. Januar 1988 im Jazzclub Hannover statt. Danach habe ich ihn nicht mehr gesehen. Ich erinnere mich an Chet als an einen ruhigen, sanft sprechenden Menschen, geradeheraus und warmherzig. Ich könnte auch von seiner dunklen Seite erzählen, den Drogengeschichten, aber das haben schon genug Leute getan.

Rocky Knauer
Antwerpen (B)/Riverside · Oct 18, 1987
Jacky Lepage

Nancy (F) · Oct 20, 1987

Philppe Cibille

CB + Charlie Haden
Roma (I)/CMC Studio · Nov 11, 1987
Fabrizio Biamonte

Rennes (F) · Nov 19, 1987
136 *Richard Dumas*

CB + Diane Vavra
Rennes (F) · Nov 19, 1987
Richard Dumas

Bertrand Fevre + CB
Paris (F) · Nov 25, 1987
138   *José Madani*

Michelle + CB
Paris (F) · Nov 25, 1987
Ariane Smolderen

139

On the set of "Chet's Romance"
Alain Jean-Marie, CB, George Brown,
Riccardo Del Fra
Paris (F) · Nov 25, 1987
José Madani

Rocky Knauer, CB, George Brown
Hamburg (D)/Fabrik · Dec 18, 1987
Michael Steen

Frankfurt (D)/Jazzkeller · Dec 19, 1987
Thomas Stolper

Ich hab's überstanden. Ich hab's geschafft zu überleben, und natürlich hatte ich Diane fast das ganze Jahr über bei mir, das war auch ein Geschenk, für das man wirklich dankbar sein muß – und ich hoffe nur, daß 88 . . . Es muß nicht unbedingt besser werden, doch wenn alles so gut bleibt wie 87, dann bin ich schon zufrieden.

I got through it. I managed to survive and of course I've had Diane with me almost all this year, and that was another gift that a man can really appreciate – and I just hope that '88 will . . . It doesn't have to get any better but if it just stays as good as '87, it'll be fine.

Übersetzung: Caroline Mähl

Chet Baker in einem Interview, aufgenommen in „De Kroeg" in Amsterdam, Silvester 1987/1988

Chet Baker in an interview recorded in Amsterdam at the "De Kroeg" club on New Year's Eve 1987/1988

1 9 8 8

Chet On Poetry
(I) Novus BMG Italy PD 74347

Chet Baker – tp, voc
Nicola Stilo – fl, p, synth, g
Enzo Pietropaoli – b on 2, 3, 5, 6
Roberto Gatto – dr on 2, 3, 5, 6
Alfredo Minotti – perc, backvoc on 2, 3, 5
Carla Marcotulli – backvoc on 2, 5
Diane Vavra – voice on 8
Paul Cantos – fl on 8

Roma (I), Jan 1988
1 In a sentimental mood
2 The party is over
3 With sadness
4 Like the precedent
5 Deep arabesques
6 Chet's Blues
7 Almost blue
8 Waiting for Chet

Chet Baker in Europe
(D) b&w bwcd 001

Chet Baker – tp on 11

København (DK), Jan 29, 1988
9 Interview with Ib Skovgaard
10 Interview with Leonard Malone
11 I remember Clifford

Jan Erik Vold & Chet Baker
Blåmann! Blåmann!
(N) Hot Club Records HCRCD 50

Chet Baker – tp, voc on 11
Jan Erik Vold – lyrics, voice
Egil Kapstad – p
Philip Catherine – g
Terje Venaas – b

Paris (F), Feb 17/18, 1988
1 Et nytt møte [Blåmann, Blåmann]
2 In memory of [If you could see me now]
   I: Den svimle svingen
   II: Der bjørketreet stod
   III: En trane letter
3 Balladen om smørblid
4 I går ja
5 Jeg ser [Children's Waltz]
6 At fuglene ikke synger [Skylark]
7 Elg [Makin' whopee]
8 Wigwam [Body and soul]
9 Fuglen fra kapingamarangi
10 6 Hekt [Love for sale]
11 Koan for en Kulturbyråkrat
   [How high the moon]
12 Furukonglesang [Alice in wonderland]
13 Ingefærblomstenes duft
   [My foolish heart]
15 Uten ord, fire island
   [I want a little girl]

Chet Baker & Enrico Pieranunzi
The Heart Of The Ballad
(I) Philology W 20.2

Chet Baker – tp, voc on 4, 5, 7, 8, 10
Enrico Pieranunzi – p

Recanati (I), Feb 29, 1988
1 But Beautiful (take 1/it)
2 But Beautiful (take 2)
3 But Beautiful (take 3/it)
4 My old flame
5 The thrill is gone
6 Here's that rainy day
7 If you could see me now
8 All the way
9 But Beautiful (take 4)
10 Darn that dream

Chet Baker & Space Jazz Trio
Little Girl Blue
(I) Philology W 21.2

Chet Baker – tp, voc on 6
Enrico Pieranunzi – p
Enzo Pietropaoli – b
Fabrizio Sferra – dr

Recanati (I), March 1/2, 1988
1 I thought about you
2 Come rain or come shine
3 Blue in green
4 House of Jade
5 Old devil moon
6 Little girl blue
7 Just one of those things

Archie Shepp & Chet Baker
In Memory Of
(D) L+R CDLR 45006
(USA) Optimism 50069

Chet Baker – tp, voc on 2, 7
Archie Shepp – ts, voc on 1
Horace Parlan – p
Herman Wright – b
Clifford Jarvis – dr

Frankfurt (D), March 13, 1988
1 Dedication to Bessie Smith's Blues
2 My foolish heart
3 Confirmation

Paris (F), March 14, 1988
4 When lights are low
5 How deep is the ocean
6 Old devil moon
7 My ideal

Nino Buonocore
Una Città Tra Le Mani
(I) EMI 090-7902042

Nino Buonocore – voc, g
Chet Baker – tp
James Tenese – ts on 4
Ernesto Vitolo – p, synth
Rino Zurzolo – b
Agostino Marangolo – dr
Rosario Jermano – perc

Milano (I), March 1988
3 Tieni il tempo
4 Boulevard
6 Un po' di più

Live In Rosenheim
Last Recording As Quartet
(NL) Timeless CDSJP 233
Farewell
(J) Timeless Alfa 29R2-42
(J) Timeless Alfa ALCR-246
(Track 6 missing)

Chet Baker – tp, voc on 2
Nicola Stilo – g, fl
Marc Abrams – b
Luca Flores – p

Rosenheim (D), April 17, 1988
1 Funk in deep freeze
2 I'm a fool to want you
3 Portrait in black and white
4 In a sentimental mood
5 If I should lose you
6 Arbor way

My Favourite Songs
(D) Enja 5097-2
(USA) Rhino R21S-79600
(J) Enja ENJ-5

Chet Baker – tp, voc on 2,7
NDR-Bigband
Radio Orchester Hannover
directed by Dieter Glawischnig
Herb Geller – as
Walter Norris – p
John Schröder – g
Lucas Lindholm – b
Aage Tangaard – dr

Hannover (D), April 28, 1988
1 All Blues
2 My funny Valentine
3 Well you needn't
4 Summertime
5 In your own sweet way
6 Django
7 I fall in love too easily

Straight From The Heart
(D) Enja 6020-2
(USA) Rhino R21S-79624
(J) Enja ENJ-22

Chet Baker – tp, voc on 2
NDR-Bigband
Radio Orchester Hannover
directed by Dieter Glawischnig
Herb Geller – as
Walter Norris – p
John Schröder – g
Lucas Lindholm – b
Aage Tangaard – dr

Hannover (D), April 28, 1988
1 Look for the silver lining
2 I get along without you very well
3 Conception
4 There's a small hotel
5 Sippin' at bells
6 Tenderly

The two previous CDs also available
as a double CD
The Last Great Concert –
My Favourite Songs. Vol.I/II
(D) Enja 6074-22
(USA) Rhino R2AY-79650

Tour dates

January
4   Hannover (D)/Jazz Club
8/9   Roma (I)/Music Inn
10   Roma (I)/Va Pensiero
28   København (DK)/Montmartre
29   København (DK)
      Ny Carlsberg Glyptotek
30   Sandvika (N)/Musikkflekken

February
3   Helsingborg (S)/Jazzklubben
7   Berlin (D)/Quasimodo
8   Lübeck (D)/Dr. Jazz
17/18 Paris (F)/Studio Sysmo
      + New Morning
20   Ascoti Picena (I)
29   Recanati + Porto San Giorgio (I)

March
1   Recanati + Macerata (I)
2   Recanati + Ancona (I)
4   Bologna (I)/Music Inn
11   Madrid (E)/Collegio Mayor
      San Juan Evangelista
13   Frankfurt (D)/Kongreßhalle
14   Paris (F)/New Morning
15   Paris (F)/Preview of the
      film "Chet's Romance"
17   Roma (I)/RAI Studio
22   Castelfranco Veneto (I)
      Teatro Accademico
26   Liège (B)/Conservatoire

April
1   Stuttgart (D)/Theaterhaus
7-10 Roma (I)/Music Inn
15/16 Milano (I)/Al Capolinea
17   Rosenheim (D)
19   Braunschweig (D)/Savoy
27/28 Hannover (D)
      NDR Landesfunkhaus
30   Calais (F)

May
4/5   Paris (F)/New Morning
7   Rotterdam (NL)/Thelonious
10   Rotterdam (NL)/Jamsession
      in the "Jazzcafé Dizzy"

Diane Vavra

I don't think it's a secret that I am a musician. But it certainly was not apparent since I didn't play with Chet while we were touring. Travelling with Chet was very difficult at times because he tended to be a bit moody and unpredictable. One could easily become both emotionally and physically exhausted under these conditions. This was the case when he offered me $3,000 to play with him on the first Japanese tour. I simply was not prepared. Just as an athlete must train every day for months in preparation for a performance, a musician must commit himself to a rigorous practice schedule to be prepared for public performance. Since our lifestyle was one of almost constant travel, it made rehearsal virtually impossible. This was, to say the least, a constant source of frustration. It was during these moments that Chet talked about renting our own home, "just outside of Paris", where we could practise together, write tunes together, and just rest for six months. The other six months, of course, would be our time for touring. I had to go back to the States briefly, at which time he telephoned from Paris and described the house he had just rented for us. He was very happy. But unfortunately, because I was gone longer than expected, the other plans did not materialize.

Es ist wohl kein Geheimnis, daß ich Musikerin bin. Sehr bekannt war es allerdings auch nicht, weil ich auf den Tourneen mit Chet nicht selbst spielte. Mit Chet zu reisen war manchmal sehr schwierig, er neigte dazu, ein bißchen launisch und unberechenbar zu sein. Unter solchen Bedingungen konnte man körperlich und emotional leicht an seine Grenzen stoßen. So ging es mir, als er mir 3000 Dollar anbot, damit ich mit ihm auf der ersten Japan-Tour spielte. Ich war einfach nicht vorbereitet. Ebenso wie ein Sportler vor einem Wettkampf monatelang trainieren muß, ist der Musiker gezwungen, sich vor einem öffentlichen Auftritt einem rigorosen Übungsprogramm zu unterwerfen. Da wir fast ständig unterwegs waren, gab es praktisch keine Möglichkeit zu proben. Das war, gelinde gesagt, eine ständige Quelle der Frustration. In solchen Momenten sprach Chet davon, eine Wohnung zu mieten, „irgendwo außerhalb von Paris", wo wir zusammen üben, schreiben und ein halbes Jahr ausruhen könnten. Die andere Hälfte des Jahres wäre natürlich für Tourneen reserviert. Als ich für kurze Zeit in die Staaten zurück mußte, rief er mich aus Paris an und beschrieb das Haus, das er gerade für uns gemietet hatte. Er war sehr glücklich. Doch weil ich länger als erwartet fortblieb, ließen sich die anderen Pläne leider nicht mehr verwirklichen.

Michel Graillier, CB, Diane Vavra
Hannover (D)/Jazz Club · Jan 4, 1988
Harald Koch

Übersetzung: Caroline Mähl

København (DK)/Montmartre
Jan 28, 1988
Andreas Johnsen

On the set of "Jazz Masters"
CB + Leonard Malone
København (DK)/Ny Carlsberg Glyptotek
Jan 29, 1988
Kirsten Malone

CB + Leonard Malone
København (DK)/Ny Carlsberg Glyptotek
Jan 29, 1988
Kirsten Malone

Hans Henrik Lerfeldt + CB
København (DK) / Ny Carlsberg Glyptotek
Jan 29, 1988
150   *Kirsten Malone*

Hans Henrik Lerfeldt, CB, Terry Carter,
Leonard Malone, Poul-Henning Olsen
København (DK)/Ny Carlsberg Glyptotek
Jan 29, 1988
Kirsten Malone   **151**

Nicola Stilo + CB
Helsingborg (S) · Feb 3, 1988
Roland Bengtsson

Walter Norris + CB
Berlin (D) / Quasimodo · Feb 7, 1988
David Baltzer

CB + Nicola Stilo
Berlin (D) / Quasimodo · Feb 7, 1988

154   *David Baltzer*

CB + Jan Erik Vold
Paris (F) / Studio Sysmo · Feb 17, 1988
Randi Hultin

Ich mochte die Auswahl der Titel: schöne Melodien, einfach zu spielende Strukturen, große Freiheiten waren erlaubt; nach Details fragte er nicht, denn der allgemeine musikalische Fluß war wichtiger als Einzelheiten. Soweit es mich betrifft, so habe ich sehr häufig seine Einstellung zur Musik untersucht. Dies half mir damals und hilft mir auch noch heute, meinen eigenen Stil zu entwickeln.

Ich lernte durch ihn auch Hein Van de Geyn kennen, einen Bassisten aus Holland. Ich erinnere mich noch, wie Chet zu mir sagte: „Es wird dir gefallen, mit Hein zu spielen; ihr werdet gut zusammenpassen."

Ich erlebte eine großartige Zeit (Ende Juni 1985); ich begann, nachdem wir unsere Soli gespielt hatten, mit Chet gleichzeitig ein Solo zu spielen, wobei sich sehr schöne zweistimmige Ideen entwickelten. Wenn ich seiner Klavierbegleitung zuhörte, begann ich, das gleiche auf der Gitarre im Hintergrund seiner Trompetensoli zu versuchen.

Als „Mensch" war Chet sehr schweigsam. Doch wenn er etwas sagte, dann war es im allgemeinen bedeutsam und treffend. Er war eher ein Einzelgänger, doch habe ich auch zeitweilig erlebt (z.B. 1985, als wir bei einer Tournee durch Italien Florenz besuchten), daß er sehr gesprächig, humorvoll und sehr glücklich war. Manchmal war er unberechenbar.

Ich spielte mit ihm von 1981 bis 1988 auf mehreren europäischen Festivals. Beim zweiten Auftritt mit ihm in Aarow (Schweiz) geschah etwas Erstaunliches mit mir. In zunehmendem Maße begann ich, während des Konzertes ein körperliches Glücksgefühl zu empfinden, daß ich Teil einer so musikalischen Einheit sein durfte, wie ich sie seit langem nicht erlebt hatte.

Philip Catherine*

I liked the choice of tunes: nice melodies, simple structures to play on, a great freedom was given; no details were asked by him but the general flow of music was more important than details. As far as I am concerned I have studied a lot of approach to music. This helped me and still helps me today to develop my own style.

I also met Hein Van de Geyn, a bass player from Holland, through him. And I remember Chet telling me: "You will like playing with Hein and you will fit together."

I had a great time (end of June 1985) when I started after playing our solos, to play solo together with Chet which made so beautiful two voice inventions. And also by listening to his piano comping, I started to try to do the same on a guitar in the background of his trumpet solos.

As a "person" Chet spoke very little. But generally, when he said something, it was significant and to the point. He was mostly a solitary person, but I have known him also in some periods (for instance when we toured in Italy visiting Florence in 1985) of being very communicative, humourous and very happy. At times he was unpredictable.

I played with him from 1981 to 1988 at some festivals in Europe. At the second gig I played with him in Aarow (Switzerland) something wonderful happened to me. Progressively, during the concert I started to feel in my whole body something new, some happiness of being part of something so musical which I had not experienced since a very long time before.

Übersetzung: Margret Brown
*aus „Chet Baker In Concert"

Philip Catherine + CB
Paris (F)/New Morning · Feb 18, 1988
Philippe Cibille

*from "Chet Baker in Concert"

Enzo Pietropaoli

My encounters with Chet were marked, like his life, by a singular contrast of contradicting emotions. In the beginning, when I was a young jazz musician, there was only love, devotion and an admiration bordering on obsession, the kind of obsession that can grip you if you come into contact with someone who, more than anybody else, represents the kind of music you have chosen to follow and which moves you deeply: a legend who, more or less consciously, introduces you to basic principles of music, principles that stay with you all your life. Statements like, "It's not important how many notes you play but how and where you play them", or, "The most important thing about a solo is how it begins and how it ends."

And then his softness, his quiet way of talking and singing. Later, in the course of time, something changed inside me, something was added: the fearful realization that certain dramatic events in life can destroy, of all things, those which you most believe in.

Meine Erfahrungen an Chets Seite waren wie sein Leben von einem beispiellosen Kontrast widersprüchlicher Empfindungen gekennzeichnet. Anfangs nur Liebe, Hingabe, Bewunderung bis an die Grenze jener Besessenheit, der du als junger Jazzmusiker verfallen kannst, wenn du es mit jemandem zu tun hast, der mehr als irgend jemand sonst die Musik repräsentiert, für die du dich entschieden hast und die dich innerlich zutiefst berührt: Eine Legende, die dich (mehr oder weniger bewußt) an die wichtigsten Grundsätze der Musik heranführt, Grundsätze, die ein ganzes Leben lang haften bleiben. Sätze wie: „Es ist nicht wichtig, wie viele Noten du spielst, sondern wie und an welcher Stelle du sie spielst" oder „Das wichtigste an einem Solo ist, wie es beginnt und wie es endet".

Und dann seine Sanftheit, seine ruhige Art zu sprechen und zu singen. Später, im Laufe der Zeit, hat sich in mir etwas verändert, es ist das Bewußtsein hinzugekommen – und damit die Angst –, daß gewisse dramatische Lebensumstände ausgerechnet das zugrunde richten können, an das man am stärksten glaubt.

CB, Fabrizio Sferra,
Enrico Pieranunzi, Enzo Pietropaoli
Recanati (I) · Feb 29, 1988
Carlo Pieroni

Ancona (I) · March 2, 1988
Carlo Pieroni

Horace Parlan, Herman Wright,
Archie Shepp, Clifford Jarvis, CB
Frankfurt (D)/Kongreßhalle
March 13, 1988

158   *Ingo Wulff*

Archie Shepp + CB
Paris (F) / New Morning · March 14, 1988
Carlo Pieroni   **159**

Micheline Pelzer-Graillier + CB

Micheline Pelzer-Graillier, CB,
Paolo Piangiarelli, Bertrand Fevre,
Fabrizio Sferra
Paris (F) · March 15, 1988

160   *Carlo Pieroni*

Micheline Pelzer-Graillier

Chet war der Mann, der mir am meisten über die Musik und das Leben beigebracht hat. Er war genau wie die Musik, die er spielte: stark, großherzig, sehr elegant. Und romantisch, so romantisch . . .

Chet was the man who taught me the most about music and life. He was exactly like the music he played: strong, generous, very sharp. And romantic, so romantic . . .

Nicola Stilo + CB
South-France · March 1988
Ariane Smolderen

CB + Bertrand Fevre

Liège (B)/Conservatoire · March 26, 1988
Philippe Gielen

Walter Schmocker + CB
Stuttgart (D) / Theaterhaus · April 1, 1988
164   *Niels Schubert*

Torino (I)/Teatro Carignano
April 21, 1988
Gian Carlo Roncaglia

Dieter Glawischnig, CB + NDR-Big-Band
Hannover (D)/NDR Landesfunkhaus
Niedersachsen, Großer Sendesaal
April 27, 1988
166 *Ralph Quinke (NDR-Archiv)*

Hannover (D)/NDR Landesfunkhaus
Niedersachsen, Großer Sendesaal
April 28, 1988
Thomas Deutschmann

CB + Nicola Stilo
Rotterdam (NL) / Thelonious · May 7, 1988
Hajo Piebenga

Hein Van de Geyn + CB
Rotterdam (NL) / Thelonious · May 7, 1988
Hajo Piebenga

Hein Van de Geyn

Am 4. Mai nahm ich die Fähre Dover – Calais, fuhr drei Stunden nach
Paris und meldete mich im Hotel „Anna de France" an, wo die meisten
Musiker abstiegen, die im „New Morning" spielten. Ich warf einen Blick
auf die Gästeliste, um zu sehen, ob Chet bereits angekommen war, und
sah zu meinem Erstaunen den Namen von Marc Cohen, einem amerikanischen Bassisten mit Wohnsitz Italien. Als ich bei ihm anklopfte,
erzählte Marc mir, daß Chet ihn für das Konzert engagiert habe.
Zunächst war ich ziemlich sauer, aber als ich Chet darauf ansprach,
entwaffnete er mich mit seinem typischen Charme. Er sagte, dem Sinn
nach, daß wir alle gute Musiker seien und deshalb doch gemeinsam
etwas zustandebringen müßten. Damit hatte er natürlich prinzipiell
recht! Es wurde Abend, und wir gingen auf die Bühne – Chet, Jacques
Pelzer, Nicola Stilo, Alain Jean-Marie, Marc und ich (mit einem
geliehenen Baß, weil meiner kaputtgegangen war). Wir spielten ein
Stück, Chet gab mir das erste Solo, und danach versuchten Marc und ich,
uns nicht in die Quere zu kommen, ohne deshalb völlig nutzlos herumzu-
stehen. Aber es klappte einfach nicht, es war ein zu großes Durcheinan-
der, und ich beschloß, Marc den ersten Set zu überlassen, um dann den
zweiten zu übernehmen. Danach lief alles gut. Wir spielten, Chet
verbreitete seinen unfehlbaren Zauber, die Leute waren begeistert. Der
zweite Abend wurde auf die gleiche Weise geteilt, und es funktionierte
wieder gut.

Am nächsten Tag hatten wir frei, und Marc entschloß sich, nach
Italien zurückzufahren, um sich um seine kranke Freundin zu kümmern.
Bei dem Konzert am 7. Mai in Rotterdam war die Set-Aufteilung also
nicht mehr notwendig.

Was für eine Kulisse! „Thelonious", einer der deprimierendsten
Großstadt-Jazzclubs, die man sich vorstellen kann. Ein mit Graffitis
vollgeschmierter Kellerschuppen in einem menschenleeren Einkaufszen-
trum, feucht und kalt. Ich fühlte mich fehl am Platz in dieser Szenerie,
was interessant ist, weil Jazz eigentlich in so vielen Umgebungen
existieren kann, aber dieser Laden war einfach nur traurig. Viele Leute
waren ohnehin nicht da, und es spielten sich merkwürdige Dinge ab, mit

On May 4 I took the ferry Dover – Calais,
drove three hours to Paris and checked into
the hotel "Anna de France", the usual hotel
for musicians playing at the "New Morning". I checked the guest list to see
whether Chet had already arrived and saw
to my surprise the name of Marc Cohen, an
American bass player living in Italy. When
I went to Marc's room he told me that Chet
had hired him for the gig. I was really
pissed off at that moment. But when I went
to speak to Chet he unarmed me with that
charm of his. He said something to the
effect that we were all good musicians, we
should be able to make some music
together. Of course he was very right in
principle! The night came and we all went
on, Chet, Jacques Pelzer, Nicola Stilo, Alain
Jean-Marie, Marc and me (on a borrowed
bass since mine was broken). Well, we
played one tune, Chet gave me the first
solo, and after that Marc and I tried to stay
out of each other's way without being up
there for nothing. But there was just too
much going on, it really didn't work, so I
decided to get off and let Marc do the first
set, so I could play the second one. After
that all was fine. We played, Chet created
this unfailing magic of his, people loved it.
The second day we again split the night in
this way, and things were fine.

Then, since we were off for a day, Marc
decided to go back to Italy to look after his
girlfriend who was ill, so for the gig on the
7th in Rotterdam we didn't have to do this
sharing act any more.

Well, what a scene. "Thelonious", one
of the most depressing urban jazz clubs
one can imagine. An underground graffiti-
covered place in an empty shopping mall.
Wet and cold. The wrong people in the
wrong place. The whole scene just hit me
as a mistake, which is interesting because
jazz can move in all kinds of situations and
places but this place was just sad. Anyhow,
there weren't a lot of people, there was
some strange stuff going on with long
intervals and shady characters. It was just
the quartet with Chet, Nicola, Alain and

169

me. The music was not really there, I felt, but of course I had been lucky to experience Chet at his best at some concerts and tours in the previous year. However, there was that magic he always brought, that poetry, that beauty. After we had finished I said good-bye to Chet and went home.

Three days later I got a phonecall that Chet was no more. It was such a shock. It took me a long time to come to terms with his absence. Even now sometimes I listen to some recording, recent or not, and feel the impossibility of him not being here anymore. Him not giving us this logical beauty.

I learned so much playing with him, from his naturalness, his intelligence. Any note he played would make sense to me, there was never waste, there was never the frustration of trying to be more than one really is. It amazed me again and again how he could just pick up the horn after days of not touching it, in his condition, and just blow music effortlessly. He understood so well where the boundaries of his ability lay that he could surpass them and be FREE.

I suspected him of giving messages. A number of times he would create a strong contrast to what was happening around him, in such a powerful way that it seemed to say, "Don't overdo it, don't try to swing, don't try to impress . . . this is the way, listen! Hear the essence, be cool!"

Maybe this is just interpretation, maybe my respect for his musical power made me oversensitive but, anyhow, it worked for me! I learned that the strength of music has to come from the essence, that it is a matter of getting in touch with any note you play, any sound you produce. And that the magic of music lies in the sound and the time. Oh, that time, his time! Impeccable, natural, never pushing or pulling. Never this "modern" playing, pushing notes after the beat. His lines just flowed naturally on top of the groove.

For me it was a big honour to be close to this man, who was one of the beautiful improvisors in history. Thank you, Chet, you're always here for me, for anyone who is open to listen and feel.

langen Pausen und zwielichtigen Typen. Wir traten nur als Quartett auf, Chet, Nicola, Alain und ich. Die Musik war für meinen Geschmack etwas zu drucklos, aber ich hatte natürlich auch das Glück gehabt, Chet im Jahr zuvor bei Konzerten und Tourneen in Höchstform zu erleben. Trotzdem waren diese Magie, die er immer verbreitete, die Anmut und Lyrik seines Spiels auch an diesem Abend zu spüren. Nach dem letzten Set verabschiedete ich mich von Chet und fuhr nach Hause.

Drei Tage später erhielt ich einen Anruf und erfuhr, daß Chet nicht mehr lebte. Es war ein furchtbarer Schock. Ich habe lange gebraucht, um mit seiner Abwesenheit fertigzuwerden. Selbst heute noch, wenn ich mir seine Aufnahmen anhöre, egal, ob neu oder alt, kommt es mir unfaßbar vor, daß er nicht mehr da sein soll, daß er uns nichts mehr von dieser logischen Schönheit geben kann.

Ich habe so viel gelernt aus der Zusammenarbeit mit ihm, von seiner Natürlichkeit, seiner Intelligenz. Für mich machte jede Note Sinn, die er spielte, nichts war überflüssig, nie spürte man diese Frustration, die entsteht, wenn jemand versucht, mehr zu sein, als er ist. Ich war immer wieder erstaunt, wie er es in seinem Zustand fertigbrachte, die Trompete, die er tagelang nicht angerührt hatte, in die Hand zu nehmen und mühelos Musik zu machen. Er wußte so genau, wo seine Grenzen lagen, daß es ihm gelang, sie zu überwinden und FREI zu sein.

Ich hatte den Verdacht, daß er uns Botschaften zukommen ließ. Mitunter spielte er so deutlich konträr zu dem, was um ihn herum passierte, daß es schien, als wollte er sagen: „Übertreib nicht, versuch' nicht zu swingen, versuch' nicht zu imponieren . . . so mußt du es machen, hör' zu! Hör' auf das Wesentliche, sei cool!"

Vielleicht ist das nur Spekulation, vielleicht war ich durch den Respekt vor seinen musikalischen Fähigkeiten übersensibilisiert, aber bei mir hat es jedenfalls gewirkt! Ich habe gelernt, daß die Kraft der Musik aus der Essenz kommen muß, daß es darauf ankommt, jede gespielte Note, jeden Klang zu hören und zu begreifen. Und daß der Zauber der Musik in dem liegt, was wir „sound and time" nennen. Ah, diese Time, seine Time! Perfekt, ungezwungen, niemals drängend oder zerrend. Nie diese „moderne" Art des Spielens, bei der die Noten hinter den Beat gedrückt werden. Seine Linien schwebten ganz natürlich über dem Groove.

Für mich ist es eine große Ehre, diesen Mann gekannt zu haben, der so wunderbar improvisierte wie kaum ein anderer in der Geschichte des Jazz. Danke, Chet, du wirst mir immer gegenwärtig bleiben, mir und allen, die offen genug sind, um zu hören und zu fühlen.

Rotterdam (NL) / Thelonious · May 7, 1988
Hajo Piebenga

Übersetzung: Caroline Mähl

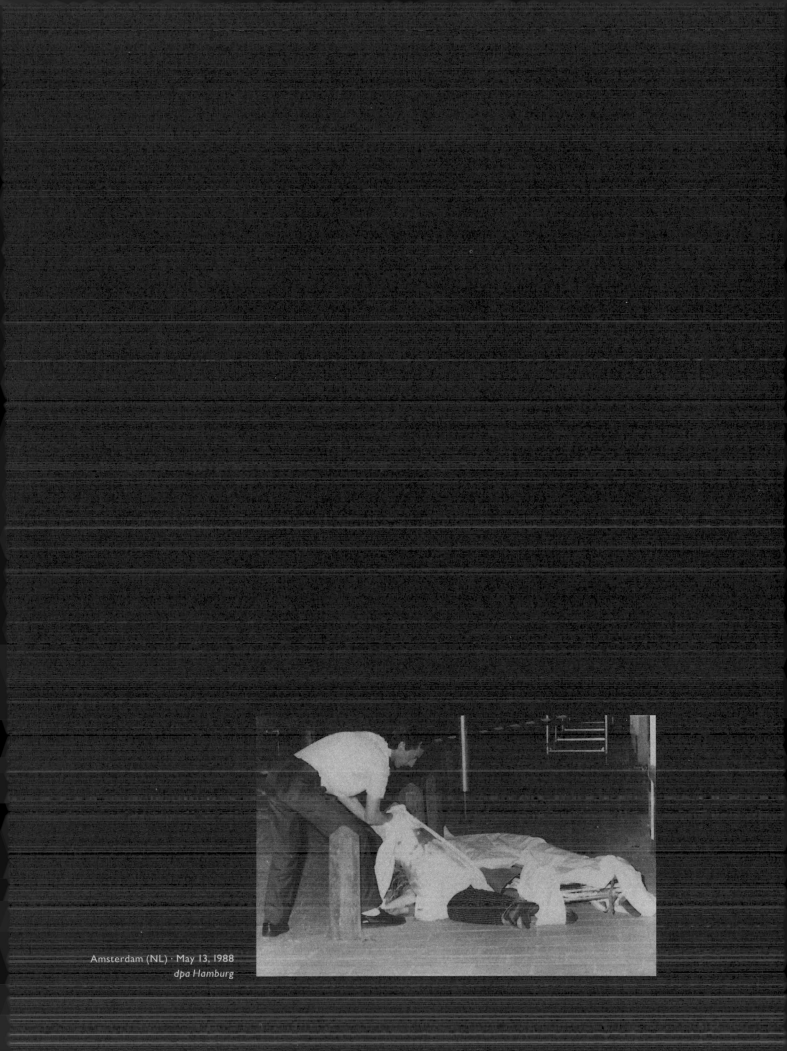

Amsterdam (NL) · May 13, 1988
dpa Hamburg

He could use the silence in his music
and in his life. He used to say to me:
"Play simple and strong."

Jacques Pelzer *

Er wußte mit Stille umzugehen, in seiner Musik ebenso wie im Leben.
Er sagte immer: „Spiel' einfach und kraftvoll.“

*from the Dutch film "The Last Days"

*aus dem holländischen Film
„The Last Days“

Chet Baker and Jacques Pelzer
Amsterdam (NL)/Uitvaartcentrum Zuid
May 18, 1988
Barbara Walton (ap)

7th Rotterdam
12 haren
13 Enskede
14 Utrecht
19 Berlin
20 Berlin
22 Hildesheim
27 Diton

3 June Bremerhaven
4 Groningen
8 Eindhoven
10 Geneva